MAKING MONEY
IN
TODAY'S ECONOMY

by
Paul Morabito

ISBN# 1-59109-547-6

ACKNOWLEDGMENT

I would like to thank God for giving me the intelligence, wisdom, and willpower to stick this project out to the end. I would also like to thank everyone who has encouraged and supported me through the entire writing process. This includes all the emotional and technical help and support I have received. I am truly blessed to be surrounded by loving and supporting people that helped this dream become a reality. Without you all, this goal would have been unreachable. I am very appreciative for all my friends and family who have trusted me with assisting them in their financial well being. Without their trust and support with their financial matters, the idea of writing this book would have never crossed my mind.

I dedicate this piece of work to all the new and experienced investors alike, that have been burnt in the stock market. I hope that this work will set you on the proper path to your riches. I also wish that after reading my literature, no one takes an investment tip and places their hard earned money into it without doing their own homework on it first. My main goal is to expand your knowledge about investments to avoid you from falling into the many pitfalls which exist in the investment world. Good luck and God bless. May all your financial dreams come true.

FOREWORD

The days of picking a stock out of a hat and throwing a dart at the stock section in the daily newspaper is now over. At last, a money making formula system that Paul Morabito calls the Formula X rating system. This system was constructed to be a guide and stepping stone for future trades in the stock market. Formula X should be used for rating all stock opportunities. Learning to rate these stocks will provide you a lucrative future in the marketplace of today. Not only will you be able to use this system to make money in the stock market, you will also learn how to combine this system with the insight and skills you already have. Spending hours at a time or even weeks on end trading on the Internet will not provide you with all the essential knowledge needed to survive the stock market. Even the most masterful of fund managers stumble at times while using basic essential fundamentals to keep their funds or clients afloat. Do not worry, Paul Morabito created a rating system that, if used, will provide needed assistance in order for you to achieve the financial dreams you may have been thinking about. Now you can stop being too afraid to attempt being a stocks and/or bonds trader. Whether you are a first time investor, or an experienced trader, there is something for everyone to learn inside this easy to read book. Soon you will be buying one for your family and friends so that they too can become successful.

PREFACE

Let me introduce myself. My name is Paul Morabito. I am a registered pharmacist in the state of New Jersey, which is where I reside. My financial education background includes both a Series 7 and a Series 63 license. My career started as a pharmacist in 1996; but my love and interest for the stock market has driven me down a new path. One day, I asked myself, "Why spend my entire life working for a single company when I can invest and own a piece of several corporations?"

The stock market has made and destroyed several individuals over the years. My goal is to try lending a helping hand to others who might care to make money in today's market. What I will do through this book is to provide you, the individual investor, knowledge in value investing. By the time you finish this book, you will also have more knowledge in picking undervalued securities for your portfolio. At the same time, I would like to broaden your horizons and cover some subjects that are interesting and important for your financial quest. Knowledge is powering my friends. The more knowledge one has the better.

Making Money In Today's Economy (MMITE) is designed to confer on various topics dealing with securities. One of my goals is to help 'You' make money in the economy for your future success as well as your immediate success. Since time is money, I will write in easy to understand terms and phrases so that you will not have to spend a lot of time trying to comprehend this book. If a topic interests you, gather more information on it besides my book. There are many sources in today's market.

I will tap into the interesting world of investing and securities but it will be up to YOU to explore it. Your future and the amount of money you make are entirely in your hands. I am only here to make it easier for you to begin creating your fortune in a new way.

I have designed MMITE in lay terms in order for you to be able to get through it quickly and efficiently. The quicker you are able to read and understand MMITE the faster you will be able to grasp the concepts which I believe are important for your success in an economy enduring economic pressures.

Every person has his or her own forte. Find your forte and use it to your utmost abilities. Gaining knowledge takes desire and time. I will put forth the effort of teaching you how to cut your learning curve time in half. As you move from chapter to chapter, you will begin to understand and enjoy the ideas and concepts presented to you. Good luck! May you gain your financial riches that will allow all your financial dreams to come true!

INTRODUCTION

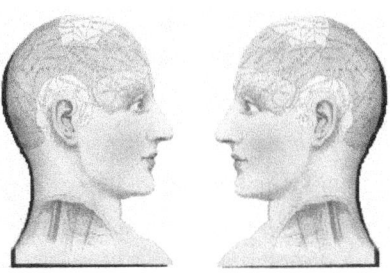

LEFT-BRAIN?   ***RIGHT BRAIN?***

TO BUY?   ***TO SELL?***

BUY MORE, OR LESS?

THEY CANNOT DECIDE CAN YOU? WHY SHOULD YOU PONDER ANY OF THESE QUESTIONS?

You can sit down now, study this book for a few days, weeks or months (depending upon how much free time you might have), and simply take advantage of my hard work. After years of successful stock trading and studying charts, books, and Internet sites, I have developed some information that creates an atmosphere of being able to become a stock trader with less fear involved than ever before.

The days of picking a stock out of a hat or throwing a dart at the stock section in the daily newspaper is finally over. Finally at last, a money making formula system which I call the 'Formula X' rating system. This system was built and being brought to you in order for you to have a stepping stone. This stepping stone can be used for rating all stock opportunities and rating these stocks will provide you a lucrative future in the marketplace of today. Not only will you be able to use my system to make money in the stock market; you will also be able to learn how to combine this system with the insight and skills you already have.

Spending hours at a time or even weeks will not keep you up with today's essential knowledge needed to survive the stock market. Even the most masterful of fund managers stumble at times and use these basic essential fundamentals to keep their funds and clients afloat.

- Need to find out more about investing? No problem.
- Need to achieve your investment goals in a seemingly winless economy? No problem.
- Need that extra cash for you or your kid's college tuition when it is needed? No problem.
- Need to purchase that new BMW you always wanted?
- Do you have any investment experience and understand the fundamentals of value investing?
- Do you know how to rate securities according to their individual sectors?

Well, if you need any of the above information you have purchased the right book with just the right formula. I am willing to share this information in a way that will make you a successful trader and you can find trading a lot easier to do than ever imagined. Do not worry. I have designed a rating system to help you achieve financial dreams you may have been thinking about but too afraid to attempt gaining. Whether you are a first time investor or an experienced trader there is something for everyone to learn. From the basic concepts of value investing to the more precise topic of day trading spread manipulation, you can tone your skills to reach your ultimate potential. Like the electrical impulses in your brain fire through your neurons, you will also fire and pull the trigger on your trades eliminating fear and greed. Once you have learned my system, you will act with confidence, knowing you have invested in the top contender of your sectors of choice. My rating system will show what companies are rising to the top and which are sinking slowly down to their bankruptcy status.

The number one problem with thinking, "If I just make this $10,000 investment, I'll be rich," is if you make decisions like that and do not know what you are really attempting, failure is bound to occur. The main problem about investing is that beginners lose more than half their capital just experimenting before they even learn the basics of value investing. Do not be one of these individuals! Cut your learning curve time considerably and learn some of the techniques of top fund managers.

FRONTAL LOBE - OCCIPATAL LOBE? All this thinking is enough to drive a sane man mad, or the average investor broke. Why take a chance? This is not a game. You do not have three strikes and your out. Once you lose your money once you are done for. Leave chance for the gamblers. You are a value investor that does his research about future potential stock opportunities.

MEDULLA OBLONGATA - MEDULLA WHAT? Just end this misery once and for all. Why use your brain for trading and deciphering stocks when you can borrow my brain and save yours and your money? Jumping into the market especially in times of an economic downturn is like trying to row upstream without a paddle. Throughout this book, begin to grasp the concepts and gain the opportunity to turn the tide. It is time for you to be the one accumulating undervalued shares for your portfolio. In doing such, you will also start to realize your capital gains accumulating for the long term.

So do not just stare at one another's brains, and blame someone else for your misfortunes like the pair of craniums illustrated here. Take your fortunes and your future into your own hands and dive into the market with confidence and authority when you make a trade. The knowledge is here. The power is there. It is your turn to succeed.

DISCLAIMER

The contents in this book are the sole opinions of Star Investment Strategies. The author will not be responsible for any loss of money due to this or any other investment strategy. Star Investment Strategies or the author shall not be held responsible for outdated or inaccurate information contained within these pages. By turning this page and reading the information within, you agree to all of the above statements. Please contact your lawyer or your financial planner before making any business investment decisions. This book is for informational purposes only, but may prove to be beneficial in providing, you the reader, with investment knowledge that may be helpful in making future stock purchases.

CHAPTER 1:
WHY INVEST IN STOCKS?

This past year has caused more attention to be paid to the stock market than has occurred in a very long time. Some stock traders have lost a good bit of money and some traders have held their own. The good news is that there are some individuals who have been able to make some money through all of this. The following information will show you that now is not the time to become intimidated. Now, is the time to learn how to 'invest smart.' This book "Making Money In Today's Economy" presents to you in a matter of fact manner just the right tools and information you need in order to help you join the ranks of stock market traders.

First, I would care to share with you why I think now is the time to invest in stocks. A couple of logical questions asked by people who are not heavy investors in the stock market are: "Why should we invest in the stock market?" Alternatively, another question heard often is; "Why shouldn't we just keep our money in the bank?" The logical answer to either of these two questions is: "Your money will not be working hard enough for you if it is in a savings account and accruing interest. This book will prove to you that your money does have a chance of bringing you a large return if it is invested in valuable stock with a good company." Hardworking people need their money to be achieving higher returns than what a simple savings account brings while money sits in a local bank. Furthermore, I feel strongly about informing you, "If you are working hard for your money, you'll want your money to be working even harder for you."

Other ways of accruing money other than traditional bank accounts that gain interest are: bonds, treasury bills, notes, zero coupons, commodities and futures.

Now to address the question, "Why should we invest in stocks?" My answer to that question would be "Smartly purchased stocks may yield far more than the current interest rate." There is also a chance of further capital gains in stock price movements. Stocks have been the most popular in our society due to their simplicity of comprehension and daily trading by the common individual.

The number one enemy for a stock trader is trying to overcome inflation. If interest rates are currently at 3% and the rate of inflation is at 5%, an individual could be constantly loosing buying power. Your money should be beating, or at least be keeping up with, inflation. The majority of stocks in the long term tend to rise on about a 12% average level. In the short term, a stock's price may fluctuate to the upside or even to the downside. However, we hope that our long time horizon will provide the returns wanted.

Speaking about returns wanted; there may be an up year or a down year. Ultimately and certainly eventually, the true value of the security shows itself after some time has passed. That is why it is of utmost importance to invest in undervalued companies. One piece of advice that is given to most new stock traders is, "Hang in there for the long term and don't get bothered with daily price swings." A big money loser for stock traders is to pull out as soon as a stock starts to decline. Many a trader has looked back with regret at decisions they made in haste because of fear.

Now, back to helping you see why investing in stocks is better than earning interest in a savings account. Receiving 10-12% returns per year on an invested amount of money is much better than the average savings account interest rate. If long term gains were not attainable why would anyone have had invested in the market? Traders just need to find some safe havens to park their money into in order to limit their downside risks. Once you have invested your money in a safe haven, you can be on your way to learning yet another investment secret that will be presented here for you in this book.

Yet another reason for investing in stocks is to be able to expand upside gains by investing in already beaten down and battered undervalued securities. Later in this book, these investment ideas will be explained and explored further.

CHAPTER 2:
HOW SAFE ARE YOUR INVESTMENTS?

If you are seriously considering becoming a stock market trader, you might ask, "Is there anything that is safe or is there a trade that is sure?" Of course, I would have to say, "In this world, there is nothing absolutely without a doubt safe or sure." This is why I feel it important to provide a few warnings to investors.

There is plenty of money to be made as an investor. There is also plenty of money to be lost. This is especially true if one has not studied some tips and investment ideas like the ones in this book. An investor should heed forewarnings from other investors who have experience at making money in the stock market. Good money management and learned diversification may help you through difficult times. You alone are the protector of your fortune. Learn how to protect your money to the best of your abilities by cutting your losses short. Allow your winnings to flourish to their full potential by practicing the methods I present to you. First, attempt to learn as much as you can by taking this task on one chapter at a time. Read other books such as this one to learn even more information and gain other tools as well. Please keep in mind that you can lose most or even all your money in investment ventures and especially, if you have not done research on the stocks you purchase.

By using the 'Formula X' section, presented later in this book describing Value Investing, I will help you to rate stocks. In addition, I will help you to learn the importance of comparing one stock to another. Formula X's real purpose is to help you to minimize losses by choosing more stocks that are appropriate. A wine connoisseur does not just go to the store and grab a bottle of wine off the shelf. He goes in and purchases a wine he knows a lot about through prior research. He is usually sure he has chosen a very good wine. With stocks, one can learn to do the same buying with the same type of assuredness.

Money invested in the stock market should never be money you need in order to pay your mortgage. Do not invest money you need for daily living expenses. Any money invested in the stock market should be the excess money that you can afford to lose. Good stock traders make certain that their stock purchasing will not place them in financial distress. Many investors who did not heed these warnings have lost their money as fast as they invested it. Careful planning provides careful futures. Another example would be that you would not be wise to take the money you need to pay the mortgage payment with and go to the race track to place bets. This behavior would not be logical for a good investor even if the bet paid off with a win. That would be more like 'luck.' I have presented here in this book a real strategy for you to use to make money that will replace the need for luck to be your only method of making money in the stock market.

Now let us take some time to look at two major companies thought to be leaders in their particular industry. Enron and WorldCom recently collapsed. Sadly, they took down many of their shareholders along with them. There are other companies as well that had major problems this past year. Can you name a few? If you are a stock trader that has been investing for quite some time, I am sure you can easily name at least one.

Enron and WorldCom both soared to very high levels in their 'hay day.' Later, their stock worth reduction showed them to be worth pennies. Many surprised and frightened investors asked, "How can we avoid this situation in the future?" I would have to answer that question with the following statement. "Unfortunately, you cannot possibly know what is going to happen with every stock purchased. Nor, can one know what might happen with every company that has stock to purchase on the stock exchange." There is a certain amount of risk at all times by all people (even the most learned.)

Let us assume you have been buying stock for a while now. Now let's also say you understand what risk management skills may be. In your particular situation, you may have purchased some stock and then traded some stock with a bit of success. Hence, you probably may feel your risk management skills have stopped you from losing your shirt. However, this may not always be the case. Some events in the stock market world cannot always be accounted for even with the most complicated of calculations or with the best risk management skills.

Recent news has presented evidence of certain companies 'cooking the books' so to speak. 'Cooking the books' means reporting inaccurate, under-inflated or over-inflated earnings or even future expectations. One positive thing that has resulted lately from the uncovering of corporate stock problems is that there is much pressure currently being placed on companies to report honest and correct numbers to their shareholders and to the public in general. To crack down on unlawful behavior many corporate officials may be seeing jail sentences in their future. This is definitely a great step in the right direction for the overall market. It is my belief that once investors feel confident that honesty resides in the stock exchange, more investors will participate. Once more investors participate; the increased activity in trading will increase the possibility of success. Individual investors, as well as the 'big guns,' must be able to regain their confidence in the stock market. This renewed confidence can bring about a bullish period and create substantial amounts of money for investors. Confidence, known as sentiment, provides an idea about how people currently feel about the market.

Stock market investors are investing all of their money strictly in the company that they work hard for day in and day out. Day by day, month by month, confidence rises, especially if no problems arrive and the company reports that the invested money is growing. Many of these employees keep investing their money right back into the company that is providing their paycheck every week. Of late, this strategy is being reevaluated. What seemed a safe idea of investing in the company in which you work is now being thought of as something that an investor should do only if he is investing in other companies also.

"Do not put all your eggs in one basket." By you using the safer method being taught in this book, you as an investor will not have to put all your money in one company. "Why is that method safer?" you may ask. To that I would answer, "This is a safer method to use because if you have all your 'eggs in one basket' you may lose all your eggs if the company you invested in goes bankrupt or is caught in illegal activities. All your eggs will fall out at once if your basket overturns.

A 401(K) plan is a very attractive financial method in which to plan for retirement. However, there is a downside to 401(K) planning. It does not need to be the only type of financial retirement plan set up for your future. One reason you should invest in other areas is to get yourself set up for multi-investing options. You need to make sure that if the company that you bought stock in sinks or takes a nosedive down bankruptcy way, you will not lose all of your money at once. Even if you purchased shares on your own in the company that you have your 401(K) in, you will have the hardest time surviving the so-called golden years if you do not have more than one money making opportunity. Not to be morbid in presentation, but funeral expenses can cost thousands of dollars. Hence, future planning is very important.

Now, we have come full circle back to the title of this chapter; "How safe are your investments?" Be careful, nothing in life certain. A careful stock trader is a successful one. Even the largest companies in the world can go bankrupt due to a loss of sales, low demand, or bad management teams. Beware of bad accounting practices also.

CHAPTER 3:
SUITABILITY

This chapter 'Suitability' will assist you in determining how suitable you are for becoming an investor. Before you make any stock purchases, your suitability, as an investor should be determined. In addition, before getting into the stock market to trade stocks, it is wise to calculate your financial position, investment horizons and goals. The following questions are ones to ask yourself in order to determine these factors:

1) What is your age category?

2) Are you at least ten years from retirement age?

3) How much money do you have left over after meeting your current monthly financial obligations?

4) Would it be possible for you to place some money away and not have to touch it in the near future?

5) Are you young enough to be more aggressive due to your lack of other financial responsibilities?

6) Do you need to invest now for your children's future college tuition and place your funds so they can grow for a decade or so, while your children reach college age?

7) Should you be careful and not too hasty with your funds and instead attempt to preserve your capital to the fullest in income producing securities?

The answers to the above questions will specifically assist you in determining if you are ready at this time to invest and become a stock trader. Take the time to determine which stocks suit your personal individual needs and goals.

I have learned that in order for my theories of stock picking to work best, the longer the time horizon I allow myself to hold onto the purchased stocks, the better. Therefore, a good standard for you to start out with is to know that the longer you can hold onto the stocks you purchase without tapping into funds put aside for your daily living expenses, the better. As mentioned in the previous chapter (and which cannot be repeated enough) never jeopardize money in the stock market that you have to keep in order to pay the cost of daily living expenses.

One of the first goals is for you to make sure all of your money and assets are in order before you begin to invest. Next, spend some time determining exactly where you are financially. Make sure you take the time to determine just how much money can be extracted from your budget before you invest. Otherwise, you will end up choking yourself financially and you might have a hard time recovering as fast as you might need. Another tip to consider is to put extra cash away that is earmarked strictly for emergencies and other obstacles that always tend to pop up in day-to-day living. The last thing a smart investor wants to do is to cash in stock in order to pay for an emergency.

Although I am teaching you methods of making good money in a 'bad economy,' I still need to inform you, "never invest 100% in the stock market." Even the top analysts in the industry today do not stay 100% invested. Younger individuals may prefer riskier stocks such as high growth securities. Internet related stocks (not recommended) also can be risky trades as they are on a high growth rate prospect.

Older individuals thinking about becoming a stock market trader may prefer a more stable means of investing such as bonds, utilities, or healthcare. A good way for an older individual to invest is to purchase a long-term CD bank account.

All in all suitability depends on a person's financial well-being or situation as an individual. Each individual is a special case. When a person goes shopping for clothing, they find that there are many styles to ponder in order to choose. Clothes come in different colors and sizes. Stocks are similar in this aspect. A clothing shopper uses a couple of barometers when determining what they will purchase. Foremost, a clothing buyer would determine how much money he had allocated towards the purchasing of clothing (think of this as your financial well-being.) A stock trader needs to use this same type of barometer.

Next, a clothing shopper would probably think about what season (cycle) of the year it was before purchasing any clothing. When analyzing a clothing purchase, it would also be wise to decide if it is lighter or darker colored clothing that is preferred. Choosing and analyzing what stocks to purchase has seasonal cycles as well.

Say you were in a desert and you happened to approach a man selling two different types of beverages in the hot sun. Picture a man holding in one hand a bottle of cold water and in the other hand, a bottle of wine. Think for a minute and ask yourself which hand you would choose? The concept of stock picking (just like shopping) must contain information about the individual's goals, financial well-being, situation, age, and time horizon in order to determine the most suitable security.

CHAPTER 4:
BUYERS AND SELLERS

The stock market is made of two kinds of stock traders: buyers and sellers. Without buyers, there can be no sellers; and without sellers, there are no buyers. To this end, it is easy to see that without buyers and sellers, there can be no stock market. For every buyer of stock on the market, there must be a seller of a particular stock purchased, and vice versa. Fluctuating stock prices bring about imbalances of buyers and sellers in the marketplace. Factors like demand, supply, fear and greed play roles in how a stock price fluctuates.

In order to trade stocks freely on the market today, there must be plenty of traders on the opposite side of any trades. In this way, when you request an order for a stock trade -- it happens quickly. The ease in which a trade executes is known as the liquidity of a stock or security. A great indicator of a stock's liquidity or ability to be traded freely can be measured by a stock's total volume of trading.

Volume of a stock is the actual amount of shares that change hands throughout a day of trading. Stock volumes are measured in terms of the average daily volumes and one goal is to be assured that we can turnover any of our holdings with ease. Our holdings normally consist of anything from stocks (securities), bonds, or mutual funds to a money market fund in our portfolio.

The New York Stock Exchange (NYSE) employs a specialist to keep liquidity present in the stocks trading on its exchange. NYSE employs one specialist per stock trading on the NYSE. For everyone making money there is someone losing it. However, differences of opinions are always present in the financial worlds of today and even more so because we are all human beings making decisions. My goal with this book is to be able to teach you how to be on the right side of your stock trades. The key to being on the right side of a trade is to know more than the person does on the other side of the trade. When there is high demand (plethora of buyers) for a security, stock prices will keep rising until the demand is saturated. When the number of shares bought reaches closer to or almost equal to the number of shares sold, the stock price tends to stabilize. This stabilization may lead the stock to trade in a narrow price range with no visible breakouts to the upside or downside for a time.

Once stock traders have driven up a stock price by their purchases, demand becomes less and less for that particular stock because the price rises. However, once purchasers stop their activities, prices will cease rising. Soon, the owners of the stock (bought at a lesser price rate) will appear in the marketplace and start to sell their shares. These sellers will end up with lucrative profits.

Regarding not buying during peaked optimism, an example of a period of great optimism is when the well-known company "CISCO" overcame (or closely obtained) Microsoft's (MSFT) market cap level. Once this occurred, the news of this fact was published in all the daily papers and was mentioned on CNBC and other news wires. This, in my opinion, was a prime example of over-optimism.

Next, there always seem to be downward trends, which can be caused by one or two occurrences. One event that can cause a downward trend is if previous buyers decide to stop buying because they become contented with their earnings. Another might be when stockholders become afraid of lowered future prices and they too decide to sell. These two occurrences can cause stock traders to jump on the sales bandwagon. Both of these occurrences cause downward stock market prices.

A good question for a stock trader to ask of a financial advisor is; "When should I buy a stock?" Answers to this question could quite possibly contain several opinions depending upon who the financial advisor is and where the financial advisor's investments are contained. First, it is my belief that it is important not to buy when a stock's optimism is at its peak. My second belief in this regard is that the worst time to buy a stock is when it seems to be over-valued and/or when the stock seems to be trading at an inflated price. Third, and much to the surprise of some people, it is my opinion that the best time to purchase a stock, should be instead, when it seems as if there is no hope of a badly beaten down, undervalued stock price rising any further. It is at this point that most undervalued situations can be found to be the best purchase.

Yes, there are companies with stocks trading at low prices. One of the reasons for low prices could very well be that the researchers did not have enough information on the company. This lack of investigation or research of a company sometimes causes the company to be undervalued. Stock of an undervalued company usually trades for great prices in the future and should be held for a long term, allowing the stocks to shine. Most buyers who had previously looked to buy this stock probably purchased all they had wanted to of that particular stock at that time.

For example, at the time the news broke, CISCO's stock price was hovering around $80/share and then by September 2001, the stock was trading at around $14/share.

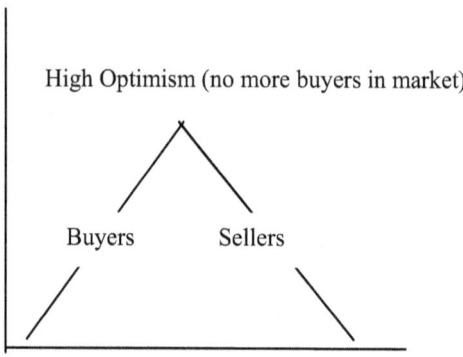

High Optimism (no more buyers in market)

Buyers   Sellers

When companies buy back its own stock, it creates less outstanding shares to be in the hands of the public. By decreasing the number of purchased shares, other numbers are also affected. Earnings Per Share, EPS, become affected. With fewer shares available to the public, the EPS value will now be higher.

Example: $\underline{\$5\ earnings}$ =   EPS
1,000,000 shares

If a company buys back 300,000 shares, the new ratio becomes:

$\underline{\$5\ earnings}$ = Greater EPS
700,000 shares

What is the importance of insider buying or selling of shares by company officials? As mentioned previously, one reason this may be

15

important is that it is a good thing to know if a company believes their stock price to be undervalued. Therefore, the company itself buys back the public's share of its stocks at a lower cost. Other reasons do exist; however, for our purposes, we will just consider this as something to think about when this happens with stocks that we own.

A. Buy Low and Sell High:

Sometimes the best thing to do is to be contraire. If as a trader, you are watching the market and learn that everyone seems to be buying a certain stock; take this opportunity to sell and take the profits if you happen to have some of that particular stock. On another note, when it appears as if everyone is selling a particular stock, you could take that opportunity to buy some of that stock. This type of watching the market and buying will help you take long positions in undervalued companies that will meet future criteria. When purchasing undervalued stocks that are falling, it is good to wait for a stabilizing price level or a support level to exist. These support levels usually form a base.

Stay away from new highflying Initial Public Offerings (IPO's.) Chances are you will buy at the top if you do not wait for the stock price to settle to its' true value. High optimism will drive buyers to shoot up the stock prices to overvalued levels.

Heavy institutional buying of an undervalued stock may indicate a turn around as well as a higher volume jump in trading. Take your time and study the stock market. With much gusto, learn as much as you can about the fluctuations described above. In general, try to look for signals that can best be done by you doing your utmost to understand this book.

One signal to look for might be when you find out about a stock buyback plan from a company itself. Alternatively, you might even hear about stock buyback plans from insider company officials. Why does a company buy back shares? As mentioned previously, insider buying of a company's shares by its officials shows that the major stockholders of the company have confidence. On a daily basis, these company officials see the business of a company through their own eyes. What they see actually can become something a stock trader watches for in order to make money.

Think about it this way: "If they believe they can make money in their company's future, then why shouldn't you?" These stocks are worth you taking the time to analyze them. Whenever a company official owning a large percentage of their company's shares make a purchase or a sale, it must be recorded as public record. These records can be found by calling the company itself, your local newspaper (for local companies,) or through a financial Internet site. Internet financial sites will provide you with a great deal of information at your fingertips.

B. Buy on Rumor, Sell on Fact:

'Buy on rumor, sell on fact' is a popular saying among stock traders. Have you ever heard a rumor that a company may beat earnings expectations? Have you ever heard a rumor that a company is being taken over by another company? Maybe you have heard a rumor that a federal rate cut is coming in the near future. What do you think that these types of rumors cause? Have you ever wondered why suddenly after these reports actually occur that the prices of stocks suddenly drop off? Sometimes all it can actually take is for a news reporter to begin to spread a certain rumor; and prices will begin to recede. Some cautious advice about these rumors (and many other types) is that one should be careful. Be overcautious about playing these momentum games -- your money is not something to be taken lightly. Instead of listening and then counting on rumors, or buying stock based on a fax sheet advertisement, invest in well-valued solid companies. Invest for years to come and not just for the future days, or even hours, like many day traders do.

Stock splits or reverse splits are another phenomenon to occur because of a decision that a company might make. Stock splits occur when a company has an opportunity to evaluate the fact that the public seems to not be purchasing their stock as frequently as the company would prefer.

A stock trading at $100 -- splitting 2-to-1 will now be trading at a price of $50. The price of the stock cut in half does not lose value because what really happens is the share quantity doubles. Instead of owning 100 shares at a $100, a person would now own 200 shares at $50.

When a company believes the public is not purchasing its shares as frequently as it would like due to its expensive stock price, they may call for a split. This split creates a more affordable stock price and makes buying and trading more attractive. Reverse splits also occur; however, less frequently. A trader who has 100 shares of stock at $50 could well become an owner of 50 shares at $100. Some exchanges require that stocks maintain certain levels of trading. If a company falls below a certain level because of the price of its stock, a reverse split may be called for. A good pointer at this time would be to avoid all reverse split stocks unless they are properly evaluated and you feel sure you can make some money by buying them. People tend to run up stock prices before a split occurs and this tends to cause the stock prices to go down or to settle later. This theory may also fall under the buy on rumors; sell on fact theory.

C. Interest Rates:

When Alan Greenspan talks, people do listen. The chairman of the Federal Reserve Board has the power to cut and raise the interest rates. Interest rate changes have astronomical affects on the market. A cut in interest rates may spur off a big rally, while a hike in interest rates might cause the market to head downward. Interest rate changes do not occur all the time; but, when rates do change, they usually effect the market depending on the expectations of the street. If rates exceed expectations, a rally will soon follow (on most occasions.) If rates fall short, watch out!

D. Price Swings:

Many factors cause price swings. The market swings up and then it swings down again. Watching your security from day to day, over every single bit of news that comes out about the economy can cause people to have ulcers. Worrying about a stock and staring for hours at ticker tapes can and will cause migraines. Ulcers, migraines and insomnia come about if there is a lot of fear involved. That is why it is so important to figure out what your suitability is. Make a plan on how much money you can afford to invest, and then do not go beyond that promise you have made to yourself. If these factors are followed, you can have fun trading instead of having ulcers, migraines, and insomnia. The concepts that are fear-based are the ones that you might have come by because of rumors. My advice is for you to invest in undervalued companies that will rise over a longer period, allowing you to sleep at night and not having to live on aspirins and stomach medications.

CHAPTER 5:
BROKERAGE ACCOUNTS

The times of easy accessibility to stock trading have finally arrived. We no longer need to speak to a broker on the telephone in order to make a trade. Financial Internet websites have provided wonders for the world of trading stocks.

If you are capable of studying stocks on your own, and need no financial assistance, then your best bet would probably be to seek out a low cost trade broker. A normal fee range may currently be $8-$14 per trade. Most brokerage account websites also have available free research tools for you to use. Take the time to investigate different features of the different websites. Not every website offers exact features. Therefore, if you take the initiative and investigate different websites, you can end up with a real education regarding stock trading. Seek out the tools offered on these websites. Begin to use these tools in order to study charts and the fundamentals of a company that you might be considering making one of your investments.

Speaking of investigating and studying websites, it is a good idea to keep in mind, when you have a question about a particular brokerage website, that there is usually someone on hand with an answer to your question. If they do not have an immediate answer, they will find an ability to assist you through another source. Brokers are motivated for you to be able to profit from your experience with their particular brokerage firm because they have the ability to make money when you do.

Internet trading may present one problem. Depending on the computer to be your buying and selling vehicle can become a negative when your computer system crashes due to computer-related problems.

At times, a problem will arrive from a high volume of trading occurring at once. One good piece of advice would be to keep your broker's telephone number available to you at all times in case of a problem. Even when all systems are working fine, there can be a slower execution compared to the 'big guns' of the business.

The execution speed of your trade (the speed at which your order gets filled) may depend on factors such as your modem speed, Internet service, brokerage firm or trade software that you are currently using. No matter what software you may be using at the time, it is imperative that you learn to use it freely before placing any real or live trades to be added to your own portfolio. Many services offer a simulation mode that may help you learn the ropes. Day traders at home may have a slight disadvantage in execution speed as compared to the software or technology that the big guns such as Merrill Lynch, Goldman Sachs and Morgan Stanley Dean Witter may have at their disposal. These traders may also have more information in front of them before they make trades due to their software. Different software packages offer different amounts of visible information that actually may be beneficial in making purchasing decisions. Investigate them and try to choose a package comfortable for you. Then you will be more likely to use the new system and you will ultimately be more successful with your trades.

Day traders fight for every $1/16^{th}$ of a point when they do business. We, as long-term value investors, will not fuss as much over a $1/16^{th}$ of a point because we know in the long term, our company's fundamentals are solid and undervalued. Not to leave you in the dark, we will be discussing how we can attempt to shave off a little cheaper price on your stock purchases by manipulating the spread of a stock. Types of Orders: Chapter 21 of this book provides more detail on this subject.

CNBC is a great channel to have on while you are trading; or, if you just want to find out breaking news. Bloomberg and other services are also available. Do not be left out in the dark.

Brokerage firms believe their brokerage account managers and services are of utmost importance. Common practice is for the firm to assign an individual account manager (broker) to you. This manager's job will be to spend time studying and researching for your best interest. Ask yourself if you would allow your money to be managed by a voice you heard over the telephone. Some people would say they would not; but then many people actually would choose this route of a relationship with their brokers.

However, it is my contention that the best way to build a relationship with your financial team is to meet them face to face. Some traders cannot tell you what their broker even looks like. It is not only more proper to meet and establish a long-term relationship with your financial advisor, but it is also very important for you to know who to get in contact with. There will be times that you may have questions about a certain security or a trade. The ease with which the conversation is held may end up making or breaking your financial success.

Next, I would like to mention another piece of advice. Before you select a broker, ask yourself the following questions:

1) Is their firm reputable?
2) Is your broker an experienced individual?
3) Can you obtain current clients as references to attest to the broker's work?
4) Is he or she readily accessible throughout the day?

5) Can you usually reach them at least an hour or so before and after the bell indicating the beginning and ending of a day's trading?

These are just some of the many questions you must ask yourself before plunging into this business blindly. Do your research -- this could mean a fortune to you!

Make sure your broker is looking out for your needs and not his. This is the broker's job and it will be up to you to let the firm know if the broker is not doing his job well.

Avoiding brokers that seem to be selling the same security to everyone else or seems to be using the same pitches to all his clients may be of a concern to you. Are his recommendations suiting your needs? If not, make new decisions based on your findings.

Many brokerage services offer margin accounts when requested. A margin account is a loan against your own holdings. This account will allow you to purchase more securities than money you actually currently have in your account. Let us say you have $50,000 of equity in an account. Equity can be either cash or your current stock value in your portfolio. If approved for a margin account by your brokerage firm, you can purchase up to two times your equity value. This is your buying power. So, a margin account with $50,000 of equity will grant you the option of purchasing up to $100,000 of stocks ($50,000 x 2 = $100,000 buying power.) You need to realize, however, that this $50,000 of extra buying power is only a loan. The purpose of the margin account is to allow you to leverage your money.

The new stocks purchased will be held against your current holdings. This technique can give you an advantage in buying more stocks just like a loan from a bank. The catch, or glitch, is if your account falls below a specific level due to bad security performance, you will receive a margin call. If you purchase more stocks than your buying power limits you, you will also be notified. The call you receive is a notification that you have insufficient funds in your account to make the purchase you are attempting. If you do go over your margin account limits, you will have generally five business days in order to deposit the funds into your account. Placing more cash into your account can make up the amount you need to cover the margin call. If you do not have enough money to cover this margin call, the brokerage firm will hold your securities and sell them off to make up the difference. Your shares of stock are now being held as collateral for your loan. The problem with this method is that now there is a debt. If there is one thing that I do not like, it is to have debt, or to owe people money.

A rule of thumb, or warning, is never utilize your securities as collateral for more purchasing power. What that activity could cause is something irreversible. If the market suddenly turns bad, you will be digging your ditch deeper and deeper with each stock that you buy on margin. As tempting as it sounds, my warning is not do this type of trading in the stock market.

CHAPTER 6:
ABOUT STOCKS

There are two types of stocks traded on the market in today's time. Common stock is the most popular traded stock. All it takes to become a stock trader is to make one purchase of stock owned by a company. This purchase will make you become a common stockholder granting you extended ownership in the company whose security you own. When buying stocks and not specifying the type wanting to be purchased you can be assured the type you will end up owning will be common stock.

A common stockholder is awarded rights such as voting for the company's officials or matters at hand, such as mergers. Stockholders are also entitled to shares of dividend payments that the company offers. A dividend payment is money that a corporation grants to shareholders for owning its stock. The dividend is usually a portion of the corporation's profits given to the shareholders as a kickback or an incentive for them to continue to hold the corporation's stock. Dividend payments are not mandatory and are usually paid out at the corporation's discretion.

Preferred stock is the other type of stock traded. Preferred stock still grants you ownership in the corporation, although you may lack other rights such as voting privileges. There are advantages to being a preferred stockholder. Preferred stockholders receive first crack at dividends dispersed from a company. Another advantage is in case of the liquidation of your company's assets, due to bankruptcy or other severe circumstances; you will be paid first and above common stockholders.

Stocks can also fall into different categories depending on each of their individual characteristics. Stocks can fall into some sub-categories such as growth, income, or another category known as growth and income. Other sub-categories are defensive, cyclical and value.

Growth stocks are examples of stocks that feed off the opportunity for growth and their growth rates are far above where normal stocks usually grow. A typical growth stock could be a company that concentrates in new technological areas of business. When you invest in new technologies, shareholders will look at the purchase based on the outlook of the company's future. Shareholders can research the technologies and then purchase based on the expected growth rate of the company. Striving for an increase in stock prices with no income or dividend gains is the main goal of growth stocks. These dividends are usually held back specifically to be reinvested back into the company so it can maintain its money or resources to grow even faster. High growth stocks can be risky during a period of economic downturn. A new technology from a competitor can also dampen a company's returns. In a bad economy, an individual must be very careful with growth stocks. Growth stocks tend to be high flyers with high expectations usually trading at high P/E's (price to earnings ratio.) High P/E stocks tend to be more volatile in a downturn than low P/E stocks. Before buying growth stocks, take the time to re-think their suitability for you.

Main goal is for growth rate to exceed the broad market.

Income stocks tend to have much lower growth rates than growth stocks. Their P/E's are usually lower, meaning that they are more stable than growth stocks. Your investment is driven more by the potential of the security to gain income in dividends for you. Less focus is placed on the potential in capital stock price gains. A best scenario would be for both to occur of course. Income stocks usually have high yields due to high dividends with a lower stock price.

An example of an income stock is a utility company. Utility companies usually have an inverse relationship with interest rates. When interest rates rise, utility prices tend to depreciate, whereas they tend to appreciate in price when interest rates fall. Income stocks are a positive approach if you are wishing to retain earnings for a retirement income. Growth stocks, however, may be more suited for a younger generation.

Growth and income stocks (perceived as one type of stocks) seem to be able to provide the best of both worlds. Growth and income rates tend to be a little lower in this type of stock, but they do actually combine the effectiveness of both growth and income.

Cyclicals are stocks that rise and fall with the economy. Cyclical stocks follow the business cycle for the sector in which they are classified. A great example of a cyclical company would be Ford Motors. When the economy is bad, there is lower demand and fewer products to be sold. In order to play the cyclical game one must know where in the business cycle they are. Timing is everything when it comes to learning to be a successful stock trader. My best advice in this regard is to buy low and sell high. A signal of great pessimism about a sector or a security may lead you to buy or go long a certain stock. Choosing a long position is when you buy a stock hoping that the price will rise to give capital gains. When a stock is purchased, in the normal manner, you will be obtaining a long position unless you state otherwise. You will find more detail on long versus short positions presented in Long Versus Short Position: Chapter 7 of this book. In a great economic boom or peak, a wrongly timed purchase can ruin you. Chances are you missed the cycle already and soon the downward trend will begin.

Cyclicals: A quick glimpse at an example of a business cycle pertaining to buying and selling Cyclicals.

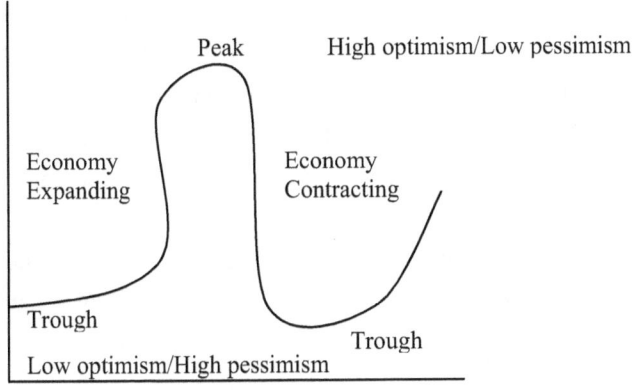

Buy at the troughs = Low optimism/high pessimism

Sell at the peaks = High optimism/low pessimism

CHAPTER 7:

LONG VERSUS SHORT POSITIONS

Two positions that a person can take in a stock trade are a long one or a short one. If, as a trader, you decide to take the long position, you will gain money if your stock appreciates in value (goes up.) This scenario is easy to understand and easy to make a decision about. Because the long position has a common sense flow to it, it is easy to decide when to trade stocks. Another way to describe the long position is to say that it is like your initial action is a buy and your final action is a sell.

When purchasing stocks, the goal and hope of a trader is to be able to sell the stock for a higher price in order to achieve capital gains. Any up-tick in price will benefit a portfolio. An up-tick is any price movement of a stock, to the upside, even by a small or marginal amount. People may have used the word up-tick when the stock market first began as a way to describe stock prices being seen on what is known as a ticker tape.

The opposite of a long position is short position. A short position is harder to understand than the long position because it does not carry with it the same common sense flow. However, I will help you to understand this position so that you can make money by using its method as well as other methods.

You may have heard the term that someone is 'short the stock.' If you are, short a stock, you will gain money if your stock price depreciates, or goes downward. The short position is like your initial action is actually a sell and your final action in all actuality, a buy. This case scenario is the opposite of the long position and it does require you to watch the market a little more in order to reap benefits from this position.

When you are short a security you do not actually own it. You are simply borrowing your own shares from your brokerage house and selling them at a specified price in an economic downturn. You can purchase (borrow) the shares at a lower price than what you originally sold them for.

To sum up, if you have hope in the stock you are investing in; or, renewed faith in the economy, the best position to have is to maintain a long position. If you are bearish (leery) of the economy or the stock you have chosen, you will maintain short positions. Bearish and bullish are two adjectives used to describe an individual's sentiment about the stock market as a whole, or with an individual stock. If an individual trader is confident about the market and believes it will go up, he is described as being bullish. On the other hand, a bearish individual is one that believes the economy or an individual stock is heading downward. In fact, a commercial exists displaying a bear and a bull showing their difference in opinion about everything discussed. They are kind of like Yin and Yang.

A great example of this is comparable to the scene in Atlantic City when you roll the dice in a craps game. If you are with the roller (or the economy) in a security, you play the pass line. If you are against the roller (or the economy) in a security, you play the do not pass line.

For practice purposes in choosing undervalued securities, we will obtain a long position in the market. Next, let us take another look at the previous chart (found in About Stocks: Chapter 6 of this book) depicting the business cycle starting at the trough. At this time, the economy slowed down and growth rates were at a low. It is in the trough of this business cycle that an individual stock trader might attempt to establish long positions. One sure way to successful trading is by learning to spot undervalued stocks in each business sector. Doing this type of research will help you to be able to take advantage of an expanding economy on the horizon.

Timing the market is one of the hardest things to learn how to do with quick success. This will take time and patience to become accurate at right timing. That is why we will take a longer time horizon and keep our securities for the long haul until they run out of steam. Now, for trading practice sake, let us say we have selected six to eight stocks. Let us also say we took our long positions in them. Time passes and the economy starts to kick on all cylinders. Two questions asked and answered at this time will help us find success. One question is "Is the job done?" The answer is "No." The second question one might ask would be, "Should we just sit back and watch the prices of the stock we bought go up?" The answer to this question is also "No." Instead, we should be constantly working to find other undervalued opportunities. The most important thing to be aware of is the long stock's value status.

There is only so far a stock can go up without switching over to an overvalued position. Remember that with each tick up, stock valuations will decline. What you may find is that a once attractive undervalued stock may have lost its sparkle and appear to not be a great buy. Later in the book, I will show you how to rate different stocks. You will learn this so you can get a better idea of how to pick a good stock to purchase. Another thing you will learn is how to spot a stock's attractiveness level early on. Keeping with our trading scenario, let us say that now the economic boom has ended; things seem to have hit their peak. Optimism has reached its all time high and everyone feels very good about all the money being made during that upturn. You, on the other hand, may know better. Like the popular saying goes "What goes up must come down." During this peak, you will want to get out of your long positions (sell) and take your profits while you can.

Let us now practice by looking at how to take short positions in the market. My advice is to be careful when taking short positions in the market. An upturn in the economy can ruin a trader. When taking a short position, an up tick in price will go against you. Let us say that our stock is at $10/share. We are currently long the stock. Therefore, we want the price to go up.

It is now question time again. This time, the question is "What are the most points I can lose given my current position?" My best advice here is to say, "If this stock reaches zero and then goes bankrupt, the most we can lose is ten points." Looking at both sides of the coin, let us say we are short the stock at $10. The question here is, "What is the most we can lose in this position?" With my answer being, "The possibilities are unlimited. The stock can keep rising and never stop." This is hardly ever the case but it can happen. Traders stuck in a short position when this occurs could possibly lose their shirt (a lot of money.)

What might be happening at this point is that the economy could be now falling apart and stock prices plummeting. "What should I be doing now?" would be the next natural question to ask an advisor at this point. My natural response to that would be, "Cover your short positions and look to go long again as you get closer to the trough once again."

Our once Over-valued stocks may be looking more attractive now to the value investor. The price may have come down so much that the stock is under-valued now. Now we can switch sides to learn even more methods. You may want to go long again in under-valued stocks and hope for the economy to expand again. This is how people make money in one stock when it goes up or down just by switching sides. Once you learn the Formula X rating system (described at length in Formula X: Chapter 16 of this book,) you will get a clearer picture of where your stock's position is in the economy. The cycle will then usually repeat itself and then the process will begin again. Formula X is a system that will use different parameters to rate stocks individually in order to get a clearer picture of their overall financial well-being. This system will help traders to spot undervalued attractive stocks that may have potential to provide great capital returns in the future.

CHAPTER 8:

SECTORS AND DIVERSIFICATION

Due to the vast majority of securities in the marketplace, we can break them down and divide them into sectors. One sector might hold many stocks that usually tend to trade as a whole. Keep in mind, there are always exceptions to this trend. These stocks are closely related in their businesses and certain events can affect them as a whole. If there is good news for that particular industry or sector, they tend to all rally in unison.

When devastation or poor outlooks is of a particular concern to one company in a sector, the other companies might all trade down in sympathy with their devastated sector partners. Again, exceptions do exist but you can rather picture them as being on the same level with one another in means of their trading rallies. They tend to fall within the same business cycle trend of one another. This is why it is extremely risky to invest all of your money into one sector. If the sector happens to be over-performing, a trader can make a fortune. Nevertheless, the risk of placing all your eggs in one basket, as pointed out earlier, always exists.

Diversification is a tool many investors use in order to avoid such a tragedy as this one. My advice here would be to spread your money out over a vast majority of companies in different aspects of business or sectors. If one security is under-performing in a sector, then you can find hope by balancing off this loss by buying a stock that is in a completely different sector. Make sure this stock is over-performing. Diversification lowers your risk potential by allowing these over-performing sectors to balance off any losses you are currently under-going.

The following is a list of a few different sectors with an example of each.

Basic Materials

- Alcoa
- DOW Chemical

Cyclicals

- Ford
- General Motors

Energy

- Devon Energy
- Schlumberger

Financials

- Citi Group
- American Express

Utilities

- PSE&G
- Nomahegan Mohawk

Healthcare

- Johnson & Johnson
- Pfizer

Industrials

- Waste Management
- Tyco

Telecommunications

- Lucent Technologies
- Verizon

Transports

- Continental Airlines
- American Airlines

Technology

- Intel
- Microsoft

CHAPTER 9:

HOW TO MAKE MONEY IN A BAD ECONOMY

Picking stocks seems to be a great challenge these days in our time of uncertainty and economic slowdown. Fear and greed also play a major role in the movement of a stock, as well as sectors as a whole. International or current events such as war or natural disasters may also drastically affect the portfolio you are working hard at building. We are in unstable times my friends. The solution to the ability to trade stocks in a stable way is the message presented in "Making Money In Today's Economy" with as much success as possible.

Let us review the example of the wild Internet craze of recent times. Getting in early on those 'high flyers' made many people very wealthy. On the other hand, late investors realized they were caught in a bubble just waiting to explode to the downside. Similar bubbles may be avoided once you get a feel for these described methods of choosing, studying and breaking down of stocks. There is no worse feeling than working very hard for your dollars; only then to have them just dwindle away underneath your nose.

Warning, if someone tells you, "You will definitely make money buying this stock," and then you go and buy the stock without going through my step-by-step system presented here, it is quite possible you could be headed for trouble. Another warning would be, "Do not purchase stocks just because they belong to a familiar or popular company." This type of buying may also prove to be disastrous if you purchased at the wrong time, or at a high multiple. A high multiple happens when a stock price trades at many times its earnings. The higher the price range is as compared to its earnings, the more unfavorable the situation becomes.

We will learn to find low multiple situations to give us more value for our dollar. Before you know it, you will be a detective on picking or choosing stocks.

Throughout the book, I will be providing pointers, facts or thoughts listed as statements in bold print. Please refer to these at your convenience. I want you to be able to feed your mind all this information and expand on it, think it through, understand it and broaden your horizons. Remember there is usually not just one precise method leading you to your riches. Nevertheless, developing your own method of deciphering stocks using many pieces of literature may lead you to your newfound wealth. Take the time to develop your skills, by toning and sharpening them. Begin to purchase with authority and calmness of mind.

Stocks never tend to go straight up or straight down. They usually develop into a choppy trend of higher highs and lower lows.

Some stocks may trade sideways for long periods. Trading sideways is a term used to describe a stock which trades in the same narrow price range for a period of time, not making any breakthroughs to the upside or downside. I developed a checklist (found on the last page of this book) for you to go through while determining a stock's moneymaking ability in order to help you work through all the concepts discussed. Please use this checklist as a reference for picking stocks.

The main goal of this book is to help you spot out value stocks having a potential to rise in value (stock price.) I also want you to be able to maintain stable returns (dividends) while limiting your downside considerably.

A stock priced at $110 has a chance of falling much further down than the one priced at $25.

CHAPTER 10:
LOOK DEFENSIVELY FOR OFFENSIVE RETURNS

These days with the Internet age, it has become far too easy for beginner investors to get involved in trading. Many investors have made some money; but trust me when I say many more investors have lost their shirts, and shoes for that matter. If these same investors who lost their shirts had known to research and investigate the companies in which they placed their trust, they may have made money instead. In addition, if they had applied Formula X to their trading, the probability of them making even more money could have been higher.

Whether the economy is pumping on all cylinders or just puffing smoke, certain sectors are used or consumed by individuals no matter what the outlook. Food securities is one sector that rises to the top of my list. We all know that people have to eat. Sure, these stocks are not the ones that come to mind first when you talk about the high flyers of the Internet age. However, most of them have withstood the bursting of bubbles in bad economic times. Food securities usually provide consistent long-term returns during economic slowdowns. I am sure by this time, you can think of other defensive sectors. The next sector that comes to my mind is beverage companies.

What I would suggest is that you research and study as much information as possible in order to find as much data on different sectors. Pick one type of industry and use it to do your first investigation on; then take and break them down one by one analyzing each company in order to apply what you are learning in this book. As you break them down, choose the one you believe is outstanding in that sector. Make sure the stocks chosen are suitable for you before purchasing them.

Utilities, the Healthcare Industry, and Pharmaceuticals are the top three defensive play stocks.

Automobile and steel stocks, as well as basic material companies are what we call cyclical stocks. These stocks usually move with the economy's business cycle. In a bad economy, these companies may suffer for long periods until the next boom or business cycle elevation occurs.

Good advice for a trader is to hunt down a stock that appears to be 'on sale' or trading at a discount to what we believe the actual price of the stock may be. No one wants to end up stuck purchasing overpriced stocks. When this happens, you would not be limiting the downside risks and you would be decreasing your chances of upward price movements. One of the most important factors I use in searching for securities is the stock's P/E ratio.

P/E's are very crucial in stock picking. P/E's must be totally understood.

P/E stands for Price to Earnings Ratio. P/E is the securities price as it relates to the company's earnings. A stock trading at $30 for example that earns $3 a share has a P/E of $10.

$$\frac{\$30.00 \text{ price}}{\$3.00 \text{ earnings}} = \$10.00 \text{ P/E}$$

The above stock is trading at a multiple of ten times its earnings. Successful traders prefer to have stocks with lower P/E's than higher ones in my theory. I ask you, "Would you rather own a company trading at 10 times earnings or 100 times earnings?" Everyone would answer this question by a majority of people saying, "I would rather the company be trading at 10 times earnings when purchased; therefore, giving me an undervalued situation with more room for my stock price to flourish upward."

Most Internet stocks were trading well above a P/E of 100 for a time. High P/E stocks will not limit your downside risk at all. You want to be as close to the true value or **under** it at your purchase time as much as possible. Picking low P/E stocks provides room for more earning power of your money.

Let us take a moment to look at this scenario. Two stocks are at $20. One stock has a P/E of $10, the other of $30. In which of these stocks do you control more of the company's earnings for your dollar value? In a downturn of the economy, the $10 P/E stock may have a shorter way down to go than its $30 P/E counter partner.

CHAPTER 11:
INVEST IN WHAT YOU KNOW

Before attempting to invest even a penny of your capital in the stock market, it is a good idea to know more about the company you want to invest in. Investigate and research to find out how the company you are interested in operates. Let us take the cattle business and research that a bit. Everyone knows a cattle herder may not know much about semiconductors. What a cattle herder does know more about is cattle commodities.

For example, you want to invest in XYZ Corporation and you already know XYZ sells telephones. The next step would be to familiarize yourself with all the products and services supplied by that company. When you do, you will find that XYZ also sells tape recorders and fax machines. Information of this nature most times makes the stock more attractive. I hope that you will now see that XYZ does reach a larger audience because it has more products. Once you have researched and realized this information, keep in mind, it is only the beginning.

Next, determine XYZ's competitors, their service types, and their clients (if possible.) At this time, ask yourself some of the following essential questions about the company and its product, competitor and services. Is XYZ in a better position in business than their competitors? Does XYZ offer superior services for their industry? If this is true, to whom do they offer the services? During your investigation, continue to ask yourself if XYZ stands behind its products 100%. Find out if their product serves a small population's demands. While studying XYZ, you may also find out that they have a vast audience making its potential limitless for growth. This is wonderful information for you to use in order to determine the amount of stock that you want to purchase.

Here are a few other pertinent questions to ask yourself as you study XYZ. Does XYZ have a management team that is far superior to its rivals or is it poorly organized? Does XYZ have a good financial background or do they seem to invest poorly? Does XYZ have enough cash on hand to perform acquisitions or is it highly in debt and struggling to turn over a profit? Does XYZ have enough of the market share of their industry; or, is XYZ finding that they are losing ground to their competitors? These questions could go on and on. I could probably fill an entire page with examples. Once you have been trading by following my system, you will be able to create your own questions.

It is my belief that the main point to get across to stock traders is to prepare yourself. Arrive at the point where you are able to understand what is going on with your investments. You do not have to be a specialist in the particular field or industry in which you invest. Nevertheless, it is vital that you understand its services and products. Make sure you pick leaders in their fields. Try to pick a company that you believe will be a dominant force in the future in its sector either by its growing profits or by new technologies.

Research and development is a great area in which to invest some funds. A technological or chemical breakthrough could actually send your stocks skyrocketing. If you have an older company that does not perform research, you cannot expect spectacular growth beyond its highs unless a great boom in the economy occurs. A rule that I would like to pass on to you is not to invest in hype. Fads and gimmicks pass us by year after year. You must make sure you do not get tricked into owning one of these so called 'fad' companies. They will only inflate to extraordinary prices and then be a penny stock once its fad or demand is gone. In my opinion, I would not buy stock in a company without a solid product that is already developed or currently selling in the marketplace. It is good however to invest in a company that has a product and invests in research and development as well in order to grow further.   Some biotechnology companies or research companies may trade only on hype or the chance of a future breakthrough product that will come to the marketplace in future years.

While following my method of investing in stock and securities, investing in chance is not exactly what I want you to learn. My advice will instead lead you toward investments made in solid companies with earnings, products and services that are already available to the public. A broad perspective is critical when the market takes its wild rides; therefore, the more you study and learn the broader your perspective.

As mentioned in the preface, I am a registered pharmacist in the state of New Jersey. Due to my vast knowledge of medications and their use and popularity in the marketplace, it would be wise for me to invest in the pharmaceutical sector.   Nevertheless, because of this knowledge, I also know other product competition exists. To go one step further, I actually fill prescriptions for these companies and know what physicians are requesting during particular periods. For purposes of providing you a clear example, here are a few questions needing answers. Has one pharmaceutical company lost favor to others? Is a new competitor's product or services taking away market share from the company I am thinking of investing my money in? Is the company I want to invest in finding itself in danger of losing its patents? Is there one particular company that is going to lose a vast majority of its past income to generic companies that seem to be flooding the marketplace? Are production and availability of my product easily attainable or is it unavailable on many occasions? Are sales representatives pushing product from this particular company; or in other words, are my competitors closing in? Is the medication profile of the company I am interested in a safe one compared to the competitors or does it have more side effects which may be detrimental?

The above questions, designed and implemented by myself, will help you to be able to see how important it is to familiarize yourself with as many facts as you can on the company you choose to invest in. As previously mentioned, you do not have to be an expert in a field. However, please take the time to be familiar with your company's product and management team.

Maybe you are a pilot and have a vast knowledge in the aircraft industry. On the other hand, maybe you are a computer programmer and have great knowledge in new software products coming to the marketplace. You also could be a steelworker who has seen a higher demand for steel in the recent months and are wondering if you should invest. Think these kinds of thoughts through with detail. Everyone has a strong point, everyone has talent, and everyone is an expert at something. Find your expertise and use it to make your financial goals come true.

Lately, I invested in a pharmaceutical company that also has existing products with research and development on its way. This pharmaceutical company also has a strong pipeline of future products. My belief in this type of investing leads me to advise you to pick a company you believe in. After doing so, maybe you will see that soon the market will believe in that company as well, if it does not already. This will be the fun part -- watching the companies you choose be chosen by other traders. The very company you choose could see its profits rise considerably. With the new financial education you are receiving through this book, you will be able to see profits rise.

CHAPTER 12:
THE POWER VALUE OF THE BRAND NAME

New traders who learn to search a company's trading price first will find success. This book teaches you to find true value; not only in a company's trading price, but also in the products it sells. Once you acquire more knowledge of a company's product, a hidden value almost magically appears. Soon, you will know even more about the possibility of a stock's price rising or falling. Most people do not take the power of knowing product information into consideration when making their investments -- the just pick a stock and buy. With my system, pushing the idea 'thinking outside of the box,' we will attempt to dig up value in various places and by using any method we can.

Helping you to go further with the outside thinking idea, let us say that I sent you on a shopping errand in a huge supermarket. I ask you to purchase a 2-liter bottle of soda. However, when you approach the soda shelf at the market, you realize that I have not specified exactly what kind of soda I want you to pick up for me. You stare at the shelf and see two products in front of you. One brand is a bottle of Coca-Cola and the other brand is a bottle of Newton Johnson's Cola Burst. In this situation, probably nine out of ten people would choose the bottle of Coca-Cola instead of the fictitious Newton Johnson's Cola Burst. Why do you believe this is true? Maybe we have stumbled upon some sort of hidden value that we have not perceived before.

Let me explain further. You might find out that not only can a company's stock be inexpensive, but it may also have a strong hidden value in its product because of the company's advertisements over the years. Commercials are created on purpose with subliminal messages meant specifically to sink into the consumer's minds. Another purpose for the messages is so that they continue to stay in our minds for a long time and cause us to tell other people about them (word-of-mouth.) How about products that have a jingle that we cannot forget? When you go shopping for a certain product, do you believe that product may have an edge in your mind? Do you believe when you subconsciously quickly shop to pick up an item in the store that a commercial jingle makes a difference in your purchase? You bet it does.

Another reason for choosing a particular product is that your family may have used the product for a long time. This might cause you to develop a certain sense of loyalty to a particular product. Some people even tend to have a feeling of safety with certain products that make them feel more certain about their purchase or the type of service they may receive from a particular company.

Now, let us say that two different company's stocks are trading at the same exact market price. Each company has the same fundamentals and balance sheets. A couple of questions to ask yourself at this point might be: Are these companies in the same sector? What can help me make my decision on which product to buy in this situation? To answer the two questions, you must look deeper into these companies in order to determine which stock has the most hidden value concealed within it.

For example, let us examine a couple of products. Company 'A' carries the Mighty John line of products. Mighty John is a fictitious ever so popular loved brand of a superhuman that saved the earth from destruction. The other product, carried by Company 'B' is the Puny Wilford line of products whose mascot was a known warrior in times of war. Which product would you pick up? I know these are drastic examples of fictitious products but the point remains clear. There is hidden value somewhere in the Mighty John line of products. Some of the reason you might choose Mighty John could be, that as a consumer, you can relate to wanting to buy a product that shows superhuman qualities. Maybe you are drawn to the product because of the plain outright heroism of the product's mascot that got your attention. Another reason may even be that you were pleased with the simple company logo. The truth is that all of these reasons, when discovered create value not usually calculated by mathematical means. This value does exist though.

It is my hope that by now, you are feeling confident about making a decision about undervalued stocks in which to purchase. You may even feel able to assign yourself benefit (of dollars) to a stock that you believe has a great recognizable product or service. If you have done the research and have discovered positive information about the company you are interested in, you might not mind paying an extra dollar or two for the company's stocks.

Let us take another peek at pharmaceutical products and observe the way pharmacy customers might perceive a brand name versus generic product. When a customer comes to my pharmacy for a stomach product, I might ask them which product they prefer - Pepcid or Famotidine? My knowledge in pharmaceuticals taught me they both contain the same compounds. The only difference in the two products is that one is a brand name and the other is a generic brand.

Which product, the Pepcid or the Famotidine, do you believe the customer usually chooses? To answer this question, let us move on to another question. Which product does the customer have an easier time pronouncing? You might think that question might be a funny one, but it is a good one to ask. A customer often chooses a product because they can pronounce one name easier than the other.

Take a few moments and look for products that you may be interested in and then exploit the products to their full potential. Attempt to discover an undervalued company. Next, see if this undervalued company has a strong brand name product. If this is the case, it may mean a very strong potential future in profits. You may even be able to pocket these profits by purchasing the stock yourself.

Familiarity with certain products causes them to sell, even in today's market. Sometimes, just the fact that people are familiar will keep them going on strong for years while other products get put out of business or collect dust on shelves. Knowing a company's service familiarity can also be translated into another type of hidden value. This hidden value may be worth a substantial amount of dollars to your portfolio. If you are not familiar with a company's service, which you have decided to invest in, then you might need to consider if they would actually even stay in business for the years to come. Ask yourself if the product is well known by the public. Not too many companies can claim that their product or service has out lasted the test of time.

CHAPTER 13:
RISK MANAGEMENT

In order to succeed as a stock trader, it is imperative to be as disciplined as possible. There are different ways to accomplish this discipline. The decision to be financially disciplined is one of the first decisions that a stock trader needs to make. Next, decide to preserve your capital as much as possible and you will be on your way to success. Learn to place this capital where it will grow for you for as long as possible. Cutting off your downside investments is yet another financial disciplined decision. Once you cut off your downside, you prevent your securities from running you down to the ground where they would just waste away the equity value of your portfolio. On the other hand, learning the difference between riding out winners as far as possible and letting a favorable trend run out before you run out of the stock position and sell is of utmost importance.

It may be a wise decision to come up with a bail out or profit point position even before your trade is complete. Some people may use a 20% upside mark and a 10% downside mark attempting to limit their losses and protect their gains. Depending on the individual investor, opinions may vary. If an undervalued position rises 20% and still appears undervalued, you may want to hold onto the stock longer.

The two main emotions that tend to disrupt a trader's thinking when it comes to risk management are fear and greed. Fear of losing money in the market sometimes causes a sale of a stock that took a slight dip in price right before its upward trend. If the stock trader had known this would occur, he would have held onto the stock and made a larger profit. However, due to fear, the stock trader might bail out and lose capital, taking his money elsewhere to purchase a different stock. A trader might jump out of the stock short-term before its long-term rally has developed.

Greed on the other hand, may be the culprit that takes away profits by not letting you lock them in when most advisable. Greed may also make traders jump the gun in purchasing more shares than can be handled. To work the system taught in this book, please apply control and try not to let fear or greed get the best of you.

Have you ever sat down at a blackjack table? While at the table did you ever notice how some people tend to lose right away? Have you also noticed from time to time that you will meet a person who plays and outlasts the other players even by playing the same amount of hands? The main reason this occurs is the difference between an individual's ability to limit their risk by using less money when the cards seem to go bad (in an economic downturn.) This type of player, the one who knows how to hammer their winning hands with more capital by raising their bets in winning situations (when in an economic boom) will become successful using my system.

You as the individual investor must know what the amount of capital is that you can risk at this time in your life. Being the banker of your capital and your destiny is one of your positions in life, as far as I am concerned. Protect that capital with the power that knowledge about a company will bring by doing your homework. Jumping blindly into buying stocks in a company just because someone said the stock would skyrocket has lost a fortune for many traders. It would be my bet that in nine out of ten cases, traders who jumped blindly and bought after they heard a rumor indicating 'buy now', probably did not even know what the stocks price to earnings ratio was.

Please remember, one rule of thumb to follow is do not take anyone's recommendations to buy without being comfortable yourself with that investment idea. Study what you believe the future returns may be six months or a year after purchase. Even if you do not follow the aforementioned advice, always think twice before putting your hard-earned cash into a stock that someone else entices you to buy.

A method that many people tend to use is similar to the one you might use in a blackjack game called 'doubling down.' Let us say you bought 1000 shares of ABC at $10.00/share and the stock crumbled to $5.00/share in a month. One person might be convinced they could purchase another 1000 shares at $5.00/share and lower their breakeven point to $7.50/share; thereby, increasing their chances of profitability when the stock recovers (if it in fact does.) I ask you, however, what if this company goes bankrupt and never returns back to the past levels achieved? Before you know it, the same stock begins to drop to $2.50/share. What will you do now? Buy another 1000 shares? Next, it drops to $1.25/share. Do you purchase more, or stop purchasing at this point? Riding your winners up instead of riding your losers down will help you towards a successful financial career as a stock trader. It has been my experience to learn not to double down in the market and to save doubling down for the blackjack table.

Reflect for a moment by looking at your current financial situation. This reflection could show you the risk management skills you actually have that might help you with buying and selling. Ask yourself the next set of questions and then reflect upon your answers. Do you hate being in debt? Do you ever pay for your purchases in cash? Is a credit card the only way you could actually purchase something today that cost over $500? Do you usually use credit cards for all of your purchases? Are you a stable person emotionally who probably will not end up overcome by fear and greed?

Every individual has financial limits. It is imperative that you find your own limit and stick with this limit no matter how much discipline you have to use to do so. Just like a bad addiction worsens your health and decreases the bank account, so too does going over your financial limits worsen your health. Many people have become ill and/or depressed because of a large financial loss that occurred in a short time frame.

Now, let us look at two individuals by using two different methods of investing comparisons. Let us study Investor 'A' who purchases some shares of stock and then decides to hold onto them for the long term. On the other hand, Investor B uses a risk management rule of 20% to the upside and 20% to the downside as a risk indicator mark. The investors both purchase their shares at a price of $10.00/share. The diagram below will show the price movement of the stock over a period of time.

$10-12-8-6-5-5-6-5-7-8-10-11-10-12-9-5-9-9-11-10-12-9-$8

Investor A buys in at $10.00/share and holds onto his shares not making any other transactions. Investor B buys in at $10.00/share and uses the risk management of 20%/20%, taking profits and losses at both of these mark off points. If you scrutinize the behavior of Investor A, you will see he bought in at $10.00/share and held onto his shares over a long period of time even over many price fluctuations. The shares went up over his purchase price and then went well below his purchase price. Investor A's outcome of the fluctuations was a loss of $2.00/per share bought [final price of stock being $8 ($10 - $8 = $2 loss)].

For the most part, I believe it can be very lucrative to hold onto shares for the long term. Long term gains over many years can produce great capital returns. Timing the market may prove to be detrimental in the long term. Constant buying and selling can increase your chances of lowering returns, not to mention the cost involved in the transaction fees charged to do constant trading.

Investor B on the other hand, has set his buy and sell-off points in stone. He has decided that no matter what; he will be buying constantly at $10.00/share. He also decided he would be selling off, at either $12.00/share in order to retain profits; or $8.00/share, in order to protect his capital from excess losses.

Looking at the above diagram of price fluctuations, we see that Investor B has pocketed $2.00/share worth of profits when the price moved from $10.00/share to $12.00/share. Whatever shares this investor purchased at $10.00/share have been sold and Investor B took the profit with him. Next, the price of the stock heads downward and the investor purchases at $10.00/share again. This time the trader was not as fortunate when his stock price reached his sell-off point of $8.00/share. He now has to take a $2.00/share loss in order to bring him back to his capital starting point. Let us say the market heads lower and remains there for some time. Then the market gradually starts to head up once again and reaches this buyer's in-point of $10.00/share. The stock again reaches $12.00/share and he pockets $2.00/share. He buys in at $10.00/share once again after a pull back and waits to see if he can pocket some more gains, which eventually happens once again at $12.00/share. Investor B ends up with a profit total of $4.00/share.

Then the security undergoes another late sell off and dips past $10.00/share (where the original purchase began) to $9.00/share. Then the stock dips again to $8.00/share where the trader later sells out of his long position. Taking a final $2.00/share loss at the end brings his profits to a $2.00/share advantage over this period.

Compared to Investor A's $2.00/share loss over the long haul, Investor B has managed to turn out a $2.00/share of profit before taking out all transaction fees of course. Although Investor B has won this battle, it may still be a better recommendation to obtain Investor A's theory of long term investing. A better percentage ratio of upward to downside risk may be 20%/10%. This ratio will cut your losses in half compared to the 20%/20% ratio which Investor B was using; therefore, limiting your downside risk even more.

Over the long term, fundamentally sound companies should rise to the top. Eventually, once Wall Street recognizes their true value, stocks will be trading better as well. As the saying goes 'cream rises to the top.' Every individual prefers a different trading style. Find your niche and develop as many skills as you can. There are profits to be made if you become a long-term investor or even as a day trader dealing with fundamentally sound companies. Keep in mind that our main objective is to preserve our capital and prevent dangerous losses that can ruin us.

CHAPTER 14:
THE BALANCE SHEET

One morning you wake up with a cold. By the fourth day, your cold is not getting better by your use of over-the-counter medications. Your concern rises; so by the fifth day, you decide to visit your regular family doctor. While you are at the doctor's office, he examines you in order to determine why the cold has not left naturally. The physician performs a thorough physical examination to determine if you have signs and symptoms of disease or infection. The physician also examines your eyes, ears, nose and throat. Then the nurse comes in and draws blood to see if there are any problems in that area. Once the examination is complete, the physician prescribes an antibiotic. The doctor informs you that he will get back to you when your blood test results come in from the lab. These test results are crucial to the physician in determining a diagnosis.

Just as it is crucial for the physician to perform tests in order to come up with a diagnosis about your health, you as an analyst and stock picker must determine your own diagnosis of a security. This diagnosis will come about by you studying this book and applying the system taught within it.

The main tool you will use in order to determine the correct stock or security for you to invest in will be a stock's balance sheet. This balance sheet will be your financial bible when it comes to studying stocks and securities. Examining this balance sheet thoroughly is very important. So please use this balance sheet to determine the financial well-being of the stock you have decided to buy.

Like the physician who takes his time to examine the suffering of his patient, you should take the time to determine if a company you are interested in is suffering from an ailment before you buy any stock. If you find the company has passed its balance sheet examination, then make a decision to sink your money into some of its stock. This type of stock purchase has a better chance of being a healthy financial investment.

The company's assets and liabilities will be contained in the balance sheet. By looking at the balance sheet, an individual can figure out whether or not a company has more assets or more liabilities. The balance sheet will show the vital signs of the company. After some experience has been accrued at studying the balance sheet, it will provide a clearer picture of whether or not you should believe the company will continue surviving and prospering. You will be able to tell if the stock you have decided to buy belongs to a healthy company or not.

Have you ever been to a store and wanted to purchase an item and not had enough money to pay for the item? Why couldn't you purchase the wanted item? Was it because you were broke and had no money or monetary means at all? I hope not! The problem most likely was that there was not enough current cash flow at the time you wanted the item. This problem, however, did not necessarily mean you had no money. You may have had money tied up in a CD. Maybe you have money or equity presently built up in a house you own or even in an automobile you purchased. There is always that ever-present credit card that seems so easy for people to reach down into their wallet and grab in order to purchase the item.

I have a few more questions that need to be taken into consideration. Have you kept a good credit rating? If you had decided to use the credit card, would that have placed you over your limit? Do you already have so much debt charged on the card that it is likely that you will be denied further credit?

These are just some of the many questions a balance sheet will help you answer about a company and a about your own debt. Once you answer these questions, the answers will help you to analyze if a company has excess cash on hand in order to go about its daily operations. You will also be able to determine if the company could invest in itself, or even make a bid for a takeover. One answer that might be divulged through your study is if the company picked has excess cash, but its value is tied up in assets. The analysis will also divulge if the bills or liabilities are increasing or seem at too high a level to sustain business operations for a period of time.

Answers such as these from the time you spend studying the balance sheet will provide the practical aspects of the company you have decided is best for you. The balance sheet contains too much valuable information for us to just pass it by and not use. This sheet will contain net income and net sales, assets versus liabilities information, cash flow, expenditures on acquisitions, shareholder equity, investments, research and development expenditures, inventories value and much more. Before determining whether a stock is in fact undervalued, we must start at the basic fundamental levels of the balance sheet.

Please do not be discouraged at the whole picture disclosed right away. Also, please do not be discouraged at the information you find at your first glance of a balance sheet. Just take it systematically and try to develop a mental picture of your stock's financial well being or frailty. Learn to pick a survivor.

CHAPTER 15:
VALUE INVESTING

What is value investing?   Before we determine what value investing is, we must define value.   People usually think of value in a monetary fashion.   Even so, personal items can have monetary value as well as sentimental value.   What determines the level of sentimental value of an item is usually based on the individual.   One individual may perceive an item of jewelry passed down from his family generation to generation to have much more value than what the actual market price might be.   This same individual may be willing to pay up to three to five times what the item's current market value is claimed to be.   One scenario might be if the jewelry accidentally got sold at an estate sale and a relative found out about it and then went to the buyer and said, "I'll pay you twice what you bought it for."   Yet another individual might just accept that the jewelry was sold and think of the piece as having no value whatsoever.

Each stock in the marketplace today has its own buyers acting as individuals purchasing the stock at their perceived value of the company. Just as the jewelry spoken about seemed to have sentimental value, stocks instead have monetary value.   The thing that drove the jewelry's sentimental value up was the fact that it was a family heirloom.   Earnings are what force a stock's monetary value to rise.

The relative ended up willing to pay twice the value of the jewelry just to get it back in his family.   In this same light, you will be determining how much you will be willing to pay for earnings in a company's stock price.   The main goal in value investing will be to obtain stock at a bargain price.   A bargain price will exist when you purchase a stock at a low price range compared to its earnings.   In other words, getting more bang for your buck in earnings. Many indicators will help you on your way to being able to determine value. By using all of the indicators together, it will help you to obtain an overall picture of the stock's value whether it is an overvalued, or an undervalued stock. Let us now proceed with our first indicator of value.

A.   P/E Ratio:

The P/E or 'Price to Earnings' value for a stock is one of the most valuable ratios in the business. You must grasp this concept by all means. It is very important that you understand this thoroughly in order to be successful. This value will give us a basic idea on where the company is trading at compared to its earnings per share. It will give us a valuation of our stock and help to determine whether or not that particular stock is overvalued or undervalued according to its actual earnings.

This is a tool to compare and evaluate different stocks that are in the same sector to determine which stock is trading at a better bargain price. In the future, this value will be compared to other economic principles in order to get a better indication of the stock's true value. In this business, calculating a P/E ratio can be as simple as division. Without being able to calculate this ratio in regards to stock trading, an individual would be better off going down a different path of investment planning.

The above calculation and the ones which follow are not complicated at all. Please try not to get frustrated. If you find you do get lost, confused or if you need to go over a calculation several times, try again; just stick with the system. You don't have to have a major degree in math in order to follow the calculations in this book.

Now, let us go over a series of simple calculations that will ultimately lead you to your financial goals. The P/E is just that -- the ratio of the price of a stock, divided by the earnings that are made by the company per share. Take a second and look at the figures below. Crunch the figures in your head. The process will become easier. In the future, when you perform these calculations, they should run like clockwork for you.

Price of 'Security A' = $10.00

Earnings for 'Security A' = $1.00

P/E Ratio equals: $10.00/$1.00 = 10

(P/E value of 10 times earnings, or a multiple of 10)

Price of 'Security B' = $50.00

Earnings for 'Security B' = $5.00

P/E Ratio equals: $50.00/$5.00 = 10

(P/E value of 10 times earnings, or a multiple of 10)

Price of 'Security C' = $20.00

Earnings for 'Security C' = $1.00

P/E Ratio equals: $20.00/$1.00 = 20

(P/E value of 20 times earnings, or a multiple of 20)

By observing Stock A and Stock B, you can realize that even though different prices exist between these stocks, they are trading at the same multiple to earnings. Therefore, both are equal in comparison according to the earnings. A $50.00 value for Stock B may be a decent share value price compared to its $10.00 counterpart Stock A (due to its P/E value.) This $50.00 value may be justified. Stock C, on the other hand, is trading at twice the price to earnings value. In a comparative valuation of the three, Stock C is the more overvalued security with all other factors being equal. The lower our P/E value, the more earnings value our stock price has per dollar spent on the purchase of our stock.

This ratio and all the other ones that will be mentioned further on in this book can easily be found on an Internet service. You do not actually have to calculate the ratios yourself. Once calculations become slightly more complicated, if you will use the methods taught here in this book, you can find the easiest ways of doing things. The main idea is for you to begin to learn how to get knowledge on what to look for while deciding on the company in which you wish to invest. This book is designed with simplicity in order for even beginners to be able to understand. If you prefer to gain more knowledge in a particular area or subject, by all means, look it up in as many places as possible. Remember that knowledge is a form of wealth and wealth is your ultimate goal. Knowledge can be gained through a collection of literature and the more, the better.

Look for a company with consistent earnings over time. A company with higher earnings will have a better P/E ratio. The higher the earnings, the lower the P/E.

Scan through a company's 52-week lows and highs. Chances are a company may be over priced at a high and under priced at its low. However, this is not always the case. Be careful and do the work before making quick decisions and investing too fast. Downside risk is lower at a 52-week low but it does not always mean the stock price will stop falling.

Make sure the stock you pick is not at its 52-week low when other stock prices in the same sector are soaring. By checking this information you can be sure there is not something currently wrong with the company stock you have chosen; avoid a trap.

B.   Volume:

Each time a trade is made through a day's trading, it is recorded in the stock's volume for that particular day. The volume of the stock will show the quantity of shares traded. A thousand shares traded will be simply added to the day's total volume. For instance, a thousand shares will be recorded as 1000. The volume of shares traded at a particular price is usually indicated on most tickertapes. This is often the long bar you can normally see going across the bottom of local television channel screens.

As we covered earlier, in order for a stock to be traded there must be a buyer and a seller. In order for a stock to be traded, there must be enough volume in the stock. There must be an adequate exchange of hands of a security in order for it to be freely traded. Volume is the best indicator of our ability to be able to turn shares over. You may find a number of stocks that fit our value investing criteria but they may have a low daily trading volume. In dealing with stocks that have a low volume, an individual trader must be careful so that he can trade, buy, or even sell the stock freely and at any time.

Information about volume may be found as either daily volume, or average volume and it will be tracked usually over a thirty-day period. You will learn that you probably do not want to be holding onto a stock that you cannot get rid of or liquidate easily. Sometimes volume increases in a stock might indicate an increase in stock prices to come. Volume increases in a security at a particular price level may be a sign of support (buyers,) or an indication of a sell-off. Traders normally like to see a price trade up higher when a lot of volume of the stock is found.

On a low volume day, a price may go up simply due to the small imbalance of traders in the stock. For the same reasons, the stock may also head downward. Just as a stock heading upward on a high volume trading day may be a good thing -- a stock heading downward on high volume block trading may send the price crashing down. If the average daily volume of a stock is 100,000 shares and the stock shoots up to 500,000 the next day, this stock may certainly be worth a second look. One might find out that someone is soaking up all the stock shares waiting and hoping for a rally. Information on insider buying and selling may also reveal clues on what company stockholders are doing.

I recommend purchasing securities with at least 100,000 shares traded daily for safety of liquidity.

C.   Beta Values:

We should try to pick out and design a portfolio of stocks that are stable instead of volatile. Volatile stocks may have a wider range of price swings than its counterpart's less volatile stock. Look for a stock that is least volatile compared to others in its same sector. The fewer price fluctuations we have in our portfolio, the more steady and stable our stock prices will be when situations arise that call for a sell-off. The beta coefficient is a great tool we can use to measure volatility. As with the P/E ratios, beta values should also be low. A value as close to 1 as possible is preferred, the lower the value, the better. A beta value of 2 versus a company's value of 1 may be twice as volatile in a period of downturn. Beta values by no means indicate a company's value. Rather, the beta value states its volatility as compared to other stocks that are in the same sector.

D. Book Value:

Book value is an important indicator, well worth you taking a glance. Book value provides an idea on where the stock is trading according to its liquidation price. Each stock has a certain book value. This price of the stock is usually obtained by determining a company's value if all assets would have to be sold. A stock trading at $50 would be considered over-priced to book value if its value should really be $35 per share. Book values for different stocks can be found by using an Internet access provider. A $30 stock with a book value of $30 would be trading at book value, which is equal to 1. A book value of 1.75 would be trading at 1 and ¾ times its estimated book value. Stocks cannot always be purchased below book value. However, you can get a significant idea on where a stock is trading.

A stock trading below book value may be considered a steal once the market realizes its bargain price. To catch these steals, shoot for a book value of <1. The market if all else holds well with the company's fundamentals would eventually lift the stock price at least to book value.

E. Return on Equity:

Let us do some reflecting at this point. Has it ever occurred to you to wonder what a company is actually doing with your money once you have invested in their stock? Have you ever thought that there just might be a way for you to actually see how effective your security's management is? The truth is, the more money the company can make from its earnings, the more potential you have to make money as well. Some companies give money back as dividends, reinvest the funds back into their company or do both.

Now, let us look at two companies named 'A' and 'B.' Company 'A' is content with the current growth rate of its company and decides in a period of a downturn to reinvest their money in a high yielding CD. This company may be growing its earnings at the standard CD rate at the time. Company 'B' on the other hand, due to its aggressive management either through a business opportunity or by reinvesting in its own company, can grow its earnings far beyond a normal yielding CD. Say a company could achieve a 25% return on their profits by investing, which company do you think will make the most of their resources or equity? Do you believe it will be the 7% CD Company 'A'? Or, maybe you believe it will be the 25% investing company? Company 'B' has an effective management team that knows where to put their money. If Company 'B' knows where to put their money; then, chances are Company 'B' would be the safer investment.

'Return on Equity' (ROE) ranks very high on any list. The higher the percentage, the better it's value. This number has a great impact on a stock's rate of growth. An ROE of greater than 25% is a great target to shoot for. A good investor does not settle for lower than 15% unless all other factors are outstanding. If I were to glance at ROE figures, I would not choose any that rate lower than 15%. Instead, I would learn to search for the moneymaking machine of a company that doesn't seem to be satisfied with a low reinvestment management-team.

F.   Debt to Equity:

Debt to Equity is also a simple ratio to consider. Common sense tells us that you as an individual would prefer to have low debt, or no debt. So then why shouldn't a company want the same thing? Yet, common sense also tells us that the majority of all companies have some debt in one form or another. Individuals have credit card debt.

Companies have credit card debts also. Debt should be controlled and not allowed to get out of hand. As you study the stock market, take the time to stop and investigate. Begin to naturally look for a company that is able to pay off its debt and not become overwhelmed by it. Debt to equity should be low for a good company. The company with the lowest debt is ideal for a trader.

Let me ask you a question. Would you buy a company that was badly in debt that would take your money in order to pay the debt off? Not me buddy! Nevertheless, a company that is in a little debt may even be a good thing. We as individuals have some kind of credit card debt that we may want to hold onto. We might want to pay off another debt first; or, we might be considering investing in another project instead. So, maybe there are companies trying to use this leverage of holding off payments to a later time in order to invest in itself or another particular project.

Let us take a look at a simple calculation of this Debt to Equity Ratio to get an idea of the range of numbers seen when observing a security for its debt analysis. Company 'ABC' has an outstanding debt of $1,000,000 and has an equity balance of $1,000,000. Let's see what our ratio yields when we have an equal amount of debt to equity.

$$\frac{1,000,000 \text{ debt}}{1,000,000 \text{ equity}} = 1$$

As you can see from this equation, an equal amount of debt to equity yields a value of 1. Now the conclusion can be made that the debt to equity should have a value lower than 1. As a matter of fact, you should try to attain a company with a value much lower than 1. The lower the debt to equity ratio is, the more attractive the stock should appear to you.

Here is another example. This company has its debt under control. Company 'BCD' has an equity value of $1,000,000 and carries a slight debt value of $100,000. What would be our debt to equity ratio?

$$\frac{\$100,000 \quad \text{debt}}{\$1,000,000 \quad \text{equity}} = .1 \text{ debt to equity}$$

As you can see from this example, a value of .1 is more attractive a debt to equity ratio than a value of 1. Look for companies with low values preferably under .3 (the lower the better of course.)

G.   Yields:

In considering purchasing a stock you should also keep in mind what a company would pay back to its stockholders. This money is mostly paid out to the holders as a dividend. This is money that the company has decided to give back to the stockholder rather than reinvesting it. Take note, most of the growth stocks and high flyers of the Internet age don't now, and didn't then, pay any dividends; therefore yielding 0% returns. Capital gains at that time had to come from stock price appreciation alone. For example, a high yielding stock that comes to my mind is Phillip Morris (times may change and it may not be true at the current time.)

Most information is probably outdated by the time you see, read or hear about it. Make sure that you check up on facts for yourself and do not rely on anyone.

I believe this stock has been yielding around 6%. For example, consider looking deeper into any stock yielding over at least 5%. Note, many real estate investment trusts, REIT's, yield high due to the fact that they pay out at least 95% of the earnings back as dividends to the stockholder. High yielding stocks over many years tend to pay for themselves. If you have a long horizon period for investing and do not need to tap into your money, high yielding stocks may be the answer for you.

Dividend yields can be calculated by dividing the annual dividend by the stock price. A security which pays a $5 annual dividend and which trades at $100 actually yields 5%.

Example: $$\frac{\$5.00}{100.00} = 5\%$$

This means that if all else remains the same, 5% of your original investment will be paid back to you annually. The yield may vary depending on changes in stock price. There is an inverse relationship between yield and stock price. If the dividend remains the same and the stock price rises, the yield will decrease.

When the stock price falls, the yield will increase when earnings remain constant.

Effects a decreasing stock price has then =

P/E Ratio: $$\frac{\text{Price decrease}}{\text{Earnings (same)}} =$$

| P/E comes down, making it more attractive and therefore trading at a lower multiple. |

Yield:	Dividend (same) =	Will lead to an increase in yield making it more attractive and paying out the same dividend for our fewer dollars invested.
	Price decrease	

Due to consistent changes in prices or earnings yields and ratios will change. Stay updated daily.

H.   Price to Sales:

Price to sales is a great companion to the price to earnings ratio. They both give an idea of how much you are paying for a company's earnings and sales. High value ratios can mean an overpriced or overvalued situation. Whereas, lower ratios may indicate better bargains for your dollar. A price to sales value of 5 means that you are paying 5 dollars for every dollar of sales. (P/S) Think of the P value as equaling the market cap price of the stock, and the S as equaling last year's sales value. By knowing the market price value and the shares outstanding, you can determine the market price capitalization.

P= CMV (current market value of stock) x shares outstanding
S= Sales (last years)

Note: (CMV) X (Shares Outstanding) = Market Cap

The price to sales ratio can give you a better idea of what you are paying for your stock if your P/E value for one reason or another is thrown out the window. It is there to help you confirm your value and to compare it to the stock's P/E. Consider the similarities of the two:

P/E = 10: We are paying 10 dollars for every 1-dollar of earnings

P/S = 10: We are paying 10 dollars for every 1-dollar of last years sales

A preferred value for P/S should be less than 1 and actually the lower the better. This ratio will tell us what a stock's price value is compared to the company's revenue sales. Just how the price to book value displayed a ratio of value compared to its liquidation price, our P/S ratio will give us a clue as to whether or not our price is overvalued or undervalued compared to its past revenue sales. We always want our market capitalization to be less than our sales revenue to attain a bargain price for our securities. We want the price, comparing it to the company's sales, to be as low as possible in order to ensure us a future potential growth. Growth is spurred by sales, and without them our stock price will not grow as well.

I.   Growth, P/E and PEG:

In order for a stock price to rise, the company must have a stable sustainable growth rate. A company's stock price will not increase by 30% a year if the growth rate is only 5%. If the stock price does increase by such a drastic measure with a slow growth rate, chances are it will not be sustainable and the price will soon falter. This price may have rallied due to some hype or news about the future and not because of its true value or earnings growth. A growth rate of at least 20% should be attained when searching for securities as value investments. Growth rates below this level may be acceptable if you are looking for ordinary market performance. However for the purposes of learning this system, that is not our goal.

Our goal is to beat the market indexes. The only way market indexes can be beat is by having a high growth undervalued situation in the stocks you buy, sell or trade. A concept to consider when thinking about growth is the size of the company. A smaller company can grow at a much higher percentage than a huge company with a very large market cap. A large cap stock with profits of 5% growth can translate into a 20% growth rate for a much smaller company bringing in the same amount of revenues. It is much harder for a large cap stock to attain consistent outstanding returns with high growth rates over a longer period. The earnings may still be there and the company will grow, but 35% growth rates usually do not exist forever.

Eventually when the company does become larger, the same profit growth will translate into a smaller percentage growth unless different paths are attained to further increase revenue growth. On the other hand, you do not want to invest in a company that is too small. You would be risking the chance of buying a potential stock if the company's future growth outlook is far beyond the reach of the company. The main thing to review and study when determining growth is a company's earnings per share growth. This information, once learned, will be our deciding growth statistic. The longer the history of consistent earnings growth the better. A history of dividend growth will also help yields and returns.

Take for example, Company 'ABCD' that has earned $2.00 a share. Now, let us presume that its estimated next year's earnings is $2.75. Can you calculate the estimated growth rate for next year? Develop a relationship between these two numbers to reach our actual percentage.

$$\frac{\$2.75}{\$2.00} = 1.375$$

The future earnings estimate divided by the actual earnings statistic provides the growth percentage as it compares to our current situation. We come to our answer of 1.375. What does this answer really mean, you may ask? What it means is that the company stock price should rise an estimated 1.375 times more by next year. In other words, this translates into a growth rate percentage of 37.5% (.375 x 100.) Growth cannot only be calculated for one year down the road. It can be calculated for many more years to come. All you have to do is take the square root of your ratio's answer for a two-year outlook, cubed root for a three-year outlook, 4th root for four years, 5th root for five years and so on. In the example above, the estimated 2-year earnings could be calculated as $3.10 a share. What will be the new annual estimated growth rate for the next two years? Consider your most recent number earnings of $2.00 and their target year's estimated earnings, which will be $3.25 in two years. This now brings you to a new ratio:

$$\frac{\$3.10}{\$2.00} = 1.55$$

The company's earnings will grow 55% over this time period. The estimated annual growth over the next two years will be the square root (for two years) of the ratio answer. The square root of 1.55 equals 1.245, giving you a total of 24.5% estimated annual growth over the next two years.

Once the future estimated growth rate is obtained, you will be able to project a forecast on where the stock price is heading. In the above example, if you were to estimate the stock's price for a year's estimated growth prospect (taking into account a stock price of $20 and an estimated one year's growth rate of 37.5%) you could arrive at a conclusion that the stock may grow to $27.50 [20 x .375 = 7.5; this figure equals the growth added to the $20 share price ($20 + 7.5 = $27.5)]. In fact, the $27.50 may be a fair value or valuation for this stock according to its earnings potential.

Growth rate is a great tool for price estimations. Growth rate aids in determining whether a stock is overvalued or if it undervalued. Before, when we went over the price to earnings ratio and determined a stock's P/E, we compared its price to earnings value to see if we were paying too much of a price compared to its earnings. Now you should be able to take this process one step further and compare our P/E to our growth rate. Something good to look for in a stock is a growth rate higher than its P/E value. This knowledge could provide you a tip as to whether a stock's P/E is low enough to even be the bargain wanted.

In the past, traders were unable to make P/E and growth value comparisons. One could not tell how to determine if a P/E of 20 (which may seem high) was actually a bargain due to its outstanding growth rate. Traders always knew that low P/E's were great to have. Now we can take a deeper look into its meaning when comparing it to growth. This is how we can tell if a P/E is low enough for a stock to be a bargain. If the P/E multiple is less than its growth rate percentage, it would be safe to assume that you are getting a better deal on the stock due to its lower P/E value. This provides some 'room to grow' so to speak. With this theory, it can also be presumed that when the P/E is lower than the company's estimated growth rate, you have found a potential undervalued stock.

P/E < Growth rate = Undervalued potential situation

This is the most favorable position in comparing the two. When the P/E and the growth rate are the same, or closely valued than the stock price may be said to be fairly valued.

P/E = Growth rate = Fairly valued situation

The least favorable situation exists when the growth rate is below its P/E value. This translates to the fact that the stock is trading at a multiple higher than its growth. There seems to be no room for growth here. If this situation is picked, you might even experience negative growth in the stock price. This is an overvalued situation; so, if you use it, please be careful!

P/E > Growth rate = Overvalued potential situation

Which of the following is the most undervalued stock to invest in?

Stock A
Stock price = $20
P/E = 10
Growth rate = 5%

Stock B
Stock price = $40
P/E = 10
Growth rate = 25%

Stock 'A' is the least expensive of the two stocks but do not let that fool you. Both stocks have the same P/E's and trade at the same multiple. Take a closer look at their estimated growth rates. Stock A's growth rate is half of its P/E value. This stock may decline in the future and probably should be avoided.

Stock 'B,' on the other hand, is kicking on all cylinders as far as growth is concerned. Its growth rate is two and one half times its P/E value. This stock, in my opinion, has far more room to grow.

Try to picture a stock's price as tending to venture towards its equilibrium. A stock's price may be overvalued or undervalued but in the long run, the market takes into account its true value either due to a correction or a rally in the stock.

A stock's P/E and its growth rate comparison can sometimes point you in the right direction of a stock's long-term movement. In an overvalued situation, when the P/E is way higher than the stock's growth rate, the stock's price will move down to reach this so-called equilibrium point. In an undervalued situation, when the P/E is way lower than the stock's growth rate, the stock's price will move upward to reach its equilibrium.

Something to compare this to would be if you could picture a guitar string being strung and vibrating back and forth over its original starting position (or true value price.) It swings back and forth over its' true value from overvalued to undervalued situations. Eventually the stock price will settle back to its true value or its original starting position. The key here is to buy undervalued stocks and then to sell them off once they hit there overvalued stock price.

Another way to compare the P/E ratio and the growth rate is by dividing the two and coming up with a ratio called the 'PEG'. As stated earlier, when comparing the P/E ratio and the growth rate, a higher growth rate than its P/E value is preferred. The PEG value uses these two statistics as a ratio. It is equal to the P/E ratio divided by the growth rate of the security as seen below:

$$PEG = \frac{\underline{P/E\ Ratio}}{Growth\ Rate}$$

This ratio will provide a better idea on the value situation of a particular stock. Looking at the ratio, an individual can observe that a lower value is the most preferred situation. The lower the value for this ratio, the more undervalued a stock may be. Having a low P/E value and a high growth rate will actually bring about an undervalued security. On the other hand, a high P/E value and a low growth rate will bring about a higher PEG value or an overvalued situation.

At this time, I would like you to contemplate this question. How can you decide which value of this ratio will be overvalued or undervalued? Well, the answer begins with; "Know when the P/E and the growth rate are equal, and then you will know that the stock may be at or near a fair value for the security. Let us take a stock that has a P/E of $10 with a 10% yearly growth rate. According to estimations, this stock may be at a fair price level. Using our PEG ratio, we can now conclude what we may believe is a fairly valued number.

$$PEG = \frac{\underline{P/E\ OF\ 10}}{Growth\ of\ 10\%} = 1$$

As you can plainly see, a value of 1 may be considered a reasonable value for a stock. Therefore, any values above 1 will be considered slightly overvalued unless the value is much higher; thereby yielding a larger overvaluation in price for the stock. Values below 1 are much more welcomed according to our value investing needs. The lower the value, the better the situation may appear to be. A growth rate of 2 or

3 to 1 versus its P/E would be very attractive to us. We would avoid most values above 1 unless outstanding circumstances exist for a security elsewhere.

PEG > 1 = Should be avoided because there usually is not as much room for growth. Other undervalued situations exist proving to have more upside potential and less downside risk.

PEG = 1 = Here we have established an illusion equilibrium point like in strumming our guitar string before. The value will probably fluctuate to the upside and downside of this value not making substantial enough gains for growth in capital. This may be considered as the true value for this security.

PEG < 1 = We have now discovered what may seem to be an undervalued situation. This is an attractive situation to look deeper into and I would pay closer attention to this stock. Break it down further using the other value determining methods. As long as the company's fundamentals are in tact and future prospects look good, this may be considered as a purchase. A 2 or 3 to 1 growth rate to P/E Value will yield an outstanding value PEG of .33 to .5. These circumstances do not pop up too often, but if picked out of a crowd of securities, it may actually prove to be a winner when the market reevaluates the stock.

J.   Current Ratio and Quick Ratio:

Another ratio that may appear to you when studying stocks and stock prices is the current ratio. This ratio places a company's current assets versus its current liabilities. This ratio helps to determine whether or not a company can come up with enough money to pay off its bills or liabilities. The higher this ratio actually the better. A higher ratio allows a company an easier means of paying their debts. It also allows the company to generate enough cash for takeovers or other investments.

Current Assets

Current liabilities

An increase in assets and a decrease in liabilities increase the ratio and shows that our company is generating capital. This usually means the company is able to pay its bills and will be on top of any surprise circumstance in which funds will be quickly required. A decrease in current assets or an increase in liabilities or debt will lower the ratio to unacceptable levels.

The quick ratio like the current ratio provides an idea on how one can generate cash to pay off short-term liabilities. The quick ratio takes this one step further by taking into account the inventory turnover or buildup. This is a much better indicator of current cash generation because inventory will be deducted from current assets. Who is to say that the inventory in the current assets can even be sold quickly and turned into cash?

Current assets - Inventory

Current liabilities

A decrease in the quick ratio, while the current ratio stays the same may lead to the conclusion that our company's inventories are starting to considerably build up. This situation is an undesirable one. It means the inventory is not being turned over quickly enough and this decreases cash generating abilities to pay off debt in the present time.

Below is an example of how the quick ratio versus a steady current ratio can tip us off to inventory building up:

Current assets = 10

Current liabilities = 5

Current ratio therefore = 2 (10/5=2, which will remain constant throughout)

Let's take a look at a 6-month span of inventory building up by 1 unit a month:

Month 1	Month 2	Month 3	Month 4	Month 5	Month 6
10−2=1.6	10−3=1.4	10−4=1.2	10−5=1	10−6=.8	10−7=.6
5	5	5	5	5	5

Please note an increase in inventory by one unit a month decreases the quick ratio while the current ratio remains the same. This decrease of our quick ratio versus our current ratio leads us to believe that our inventories are indeed building up.

K.   Profitability:

Profitability is a must for companies to continue their operations. Without profits, it would be pointless to continue business unless future profitability is planned or foreseeable. I would suggest that companies with negative earnings or companies with only future prospect earnings should be avoided until earnings are actually attained. Or, buy stocks in a company that has a long history of earnings quarter after quarter. Let us say a company brings in high revenues of $120,000,000 compared to its small market cap. Well that sounds great doesn't it? I would not be too sure. Now, what if I told you that it cost the company $118,000,000 in inventory and operational costs to produce that $120,000,000 in revenues? That doesn't sound as great after learning that information now does it? I hope that by now see a totally new picture in your mind.

The key in this business is in gathering as much information as possible. The more information you have the better a chance at success you will have. Without this type of information, you would have thought that most of the mentioned $120,000,000 was profits. Now with this added information, you can realize that this is not a positive situation to be in at all and you will know better than to invest your hard-earned money in this company. You must gather all this type of information so that you are able to come up with your own conclusions and forecasts about a company or stock you may be considering.

When revenues increase year after year, it is a very good sign that a company is growing and that there will be profits. This may not always be the case though and it certainly depends upon a company's operational expenses and their inventory costs. In order to determine how great a company's gains actually are please look deeper into the numbers and determine profit margins or percentages of profitability. In the example above, this company's cost for producing its $120,000,000 was $118,000,000. What was the profitability here?

$$\frac{120 \text{ million} - 118 \text{ million}}{120 \text{ million}} = \frac{2 \text{ million}}{120 \text{ million}} = 1.6\% \text{ profit margin}$$

This example shows a profit margin of 1.6%, which is not high at all. As a matter of fact, it is on the very low side. Something must be done in this situation to increase profits or decrease costs in order for the company to attain acceptable profitability and succeed in its business. You may consider companies as being light weighted or heavy weighted in costs or inventory. Companies such as automobile manufacturers cannot do without having inventory in order to sell merchandise and turn a profit. Other companies with another type of product may not need to maintain inventory levels and can instead produce, or have the ability to produce its product on demand or without high costs.

Let us now spend some time doing some comparisons. Then take a look at two different types of company stocks and then compare them. First, use the example of a car manufacturer and an author writing a newsletter. The car manufacturer is selling his product for a retail price of $27,000 and his total cost of producing this product is $21,000. On the other hand, we have an author that produces a newsletter and sells it for $9.99. His costs are only $1.25 per newsletter for production and replication costs. The car manufacturer will have higher revenue for selling his product ($27,000) compared to the poor authors revenue of $9.99.

Taking these calculations further, who do you believe actually shows a greater profit percentage based on the cost of his product?

$$\frac{\$27,000 - \$21,000}{\$27,000} = 22.2\% \text{ profit margin for manufacturer}$$

$$\frac{\$9.99 - \$1.25}{\$9.99} = 87.5\% \text{ profit margin for author}$$

My experience as a stock trader has allowed me to see that in this particular case, the author has a much higher profit margin of 87.5% compared to the car manufacturing counterpart's 22.2% profitability. The author's costs are also much lower and seem to be under control. The author is making a higher percent profit on his product while minimizing his cost substantially compared to a car's production.

Looking as deep as you can into a stock's profit percentages, operational costs, and inventory is very important. The recommended level of minimum profitability that I would consider would be at least 10%. The higher the profit, the more of a company's hard earned revenues will be kept and either reinvested back into the company, paid out in dividends, or invested somewhere else by management. To grow stock prices higher, profit margins should be heading upward as well.

Example of a Security Analysis

Let's take a look at Company 'ABC' and examine its fundamentals. This stock has a market value of $20 and has an earnings of $4 per share. The company's next year's estimated earnings are projected to be $5.00 per share.

Listed below are other numerical parameters that may be useful in evaluating this company or any company that you may be interested in evaluating:

Beta value = 1.0

Volume = 800,000

52 week range = 17.00 – 50.00

Return on equity (ROE)= 20%

Profit margin = 10%

Dividend = $1.00

Book value = .65

Current ratio = steady value (no increase or decrease)

Quick ratio = steady value (no increase or decrease)

Price to sales = 5

P/E = ?

Growth rate = ?

PEG = ?

By taking a glance at the these values, you must calculate the price to earnings ratio.

$$\frac{\$20.00 \text{ (market price)}}{\$4.00 \text{ (earnings)}} = 5 \text{ P/E}$$

A P/E value of 5 times earnings is a low value indeed. We may have found an undervalued stock. Let us verify this assumption by going deeper into the company's fundamentals. To determine this, you must look at the company's growth rate.

$$\frac{\$5.00 \text{ (estimated earnings)}}{\$4.00 \text{ (current earnings)}} = 1.25$$

Next year's earnings will be 25% greater than the earnings already achieved. This will translate into an estimated growth rate of $1.00 per share more for the year than was earned previously. Now, let us compare our growth rate to the price to earnings ratio value.

Growth rate 25% > 5 P/E

Our estimated growth rate is substantially higher than the P/E ratio. This is a very favorable situation for us. If our P/E ratio value was to catch up to its growth rate value, there would be a substantial upside potential for the stock's market value to rise.

To provide you with a good example of potential growth, let us now say that the P/E ratio of 5 rose to a P/E ratio of 20, falling in an equilibrium position to its growth rate. This would mean that our stock's market value rose to $80.

$$P/E = \frac{Price}{Earnings}$$

Example: $20 \ P/E = \frac{x(price)}{\$4 \ (earnings)}$

($4 x 20 = $80)

Going back to the previous example of 25% growth, we can calculate the PEG value. P/E = 5, estimated growth rate = 25%.

$$PEG = \frac{5 \ (P/E)}{25 \ (Growth \ Rate)} = 2$$

Our PEG value of .2 falls in line very well with our theory of being less than 1. This .2 value may prove to be a splendid find in the future.

This stock's beta value of 1 represents its similarity in volatility to the market. Our volume of 800,000 shares gives us just enough liquidity in the stock to purchase and turnover these shares. Observing the 52-week range will show a stock price that is well off its high of $50. It will also show that it is also slightly higher than its low of $17 for the year. Observing the return on equity value of 20%, we may be more confident in the management team's way of operating. Receiving 20% back off of profit earnings should propel the stock's value as long as it is sustainable.

Profit margins of 10% are an acceptable level for us at this time. Current and quick ratios show no signs of inventory level buildup at this time. You could find it positive when it looks like the security will also pay out large dividends. Not only can you then hope to cash in on the stock's price appreciation; you could also hope to receive an income from the purchase. Now, take a moment and see if you can determine what the dividend yield will be from the stock.

$$\frac{\$1 \text{ (dividend)}}{\$20 \text{ (market price)}} = .05 \times 100 \text{ or } 5\%$$

A yield of 5% is very attractive, especially when interest rates are lower than 5%. This usually is the case in recessions or in a period of economic downturn. To give you a better feeling of the P/E and an ability to see how accurate this ratio may actually be, you might want to look at the P/S comparison between the two. With both these values being equal, it may lead to the conclusion that the P/E value may be justified.

In case of a liquidation situation by this company, let us take a closer look at what the company's book value might actually be. There is a book value of .65, meaning that the stock's price at its current levels is worth approximately only 65% of its true liquidation value.

This puts the stock in an undervalued situation by 35% of its value. With these values, you can calculate the actual book value in dollars for the stock if it is not already listed.

If 65% = $20, Then 100% = x

$$\frac{65\%}{100\%} = \frac{20}{x}$$

Cross multiplying will lead to the conclusion that the stock's book value is equal to x or $30.77. To verify this calculation, multiply $30.77 by .65 in order to bring you back to the original $20 market price. This stock may now be worthwhile to hold onto for the long term.

Take the time to perform these calculations before purchasing any shares. Remember to rate the stocks according to your hunches and what you perceive to be an undervalued situation. Use your checklist wisely. Go through each of the stocks one at a time. You may even want to add your own calculations or additions to the provided checklist in order to help you examine the stocks even further. Good luck and great trading!

CHAPTER 16:
FORMULA X

First, I suggest narrowing down stock opportunities. Narrow them down to one particular sector; or at the very least, to a group that contains diversified stocks. Next, in order to be successful with Formula X, it is imperative to perform a comparison between the different stocks in a particular sector in order to rate what would be the best stock to purchase. Buying more than two or three of the same types of stocks in a portfolio is not suggested if you are going to use the method Formula X taught in this book.

About now, the usual question investors ask is; "How do I determine which is the best stock for me to buy?" My answer normally is, "By using Formula X." Formula X is a basic formula used to help keep on track while trying to determine which stock may prove to be a winner. Formula X is successful in rating the importance of different fundamental values and theories. Once you understand the basic principles behind my theory, you may decide to alter them depending on the importance of a varied rating system. Until you know the method, it is my advice for you not to alter the Formula X method. However, you may want to add or subtract values from my basic formula; thereby adding a new fresh perspective to the analysis process. For beginners, it is my belief that this system will prove to help substantially. More advanced investors may want to change my multipliers listed in Column 2.

The idea is to keep this rating system simple, thereby giving values for stocks from one to ten. Formula X will assist you in achieving your own opinion of a stock while using my own fixed multipliers and concepts. By combining these two methods of ideas about stocks, you will end up being able to pick winners. You will also end up able to weed out the losers if you follow Formula X.

The Formula X sheet consists of four columns. Column 1 lists most of the concepts covered so far. Once you study this sheet, you may want to add more indicators to Column 1. Just make sure that you add an accurate multiplier value to it that represents its importance value. The concepts already listed in Column 1 are the ones that I believe to be most important for success.

Column 2 is the Formula X multiplier. These values will remain constant throughout, and will not change (unless you decide to vary the Formula X multiplier at your discretion.) In stock analysis, it is always wise to keep an open mind. This sheet is intended to be a method of stock picking that will lead to successful trading by combining knowledge from a vast majority of ideas accumulated over time. As you can see, the multipliers below add up to 1 or 100%. We will use our multipliers to calculate X values based on our insight rating of 1 to 10 for each concept in Column 1 that we have discussed. Column 3 will be the insight rating of our thoughts on each particular concept mentioned thus far.

Keeping an open mind will help you to form your own opinion, which is very valuable for you to become the successful trader you desire to be. Do not be afraid to cast your own developing insight on your values once you feel comfortable with the concepts. This will help you to become more confident in your own stock purchases.

Next, rate Column 3 from 1 to 10, with 10 being the highest value attainable. Once you come to your own conclusions by doing your homework and by calculating values for your security, you will then multiply your value (those in Column 3) by the constant value multipliers in Column 2. This will give us our X values for Column 4.

Once we have calculated all of our X values, we will take the sum of our X values (Column 4) and come up with our Formula X rating. This will be the final rating value to use for all stock comparisons.

After you have assigned all the ratings, you will be able to see the conclusions you come up with. The most important concept to develop is a means of comparison to get you on your way.

THE FORMULA

Column 1	Multiplier X Column 2	Insight Rating Column 3	= Value Column 4
Indicator	Multiplier	Insight Rating	Value
P/E Value (P/S)	0.3		
Yield Value	0.15		
Return on Equity	0.2		
Book Value	0.05		
Debt to Equity	0.1		
Growth Rate > P/E and PEG value	0.2		
TOTALS	1		(Sum = your rating value for security)

| | Multiplier X | Insight Rating | = Value |
| Column 1 | Column 2 | Column 3 | Column 4 |
Indicator	Multiplier	Insight Rating	Value
P/E Value (P/S)	0.3		
Yield Value	0.15		
Return on Equity	0.2		
Book Value	0.05		
Debt to Equity	0.1		
Growth Rate > P/E and PEG value	0.2		
TOTALS	1		(Sum = your rating value for security)

Now begin by working your way through the checklist. Put stocks to the ultimate comparison test in order to determine a combined rating on each security. It is by this process that you can choose the upward potential stock that you took the time to determine. Just to give you a brief valuation of the first P/E value rating, I will list a number range to go by that I feel may be appropriate as a rating chart. If you prefer to do so, you may want to alter these numbers slightly.

An example of my P/E range insight rating value may be as follows:

PE	>100	= 1 to 2 insight rating in Column 3
PE	60-80	= 2 to 3
PE	40-60	= 3 to 4
PE	30-40	= 4 to 5
PE	20-30	= 6 to 7
PE	15-20	= 7 to 8
PE	10-15	= 8
PE	5-10	= 9
PE	<5	= 10

If you were to rate a stock as having a 10 P/E insight rating analysis, you would then multiply our 10 value by a suggested multiplier value of .3 to equal a value of 3 in Column 4. Next, add all of Column 4 values to equal a final total rating. Remember that the Formula X values are not set in stone. You might even want to alter the values in the future depending on the strictness or leniency at the time of making a business decision.

The second rating that the stock prices must go through is the yield test rating. I liked assigning this as a test in order to help attain income-producing capabilities with chosen securities. Sometimes dividends may actually pay off and help get you through some hard economic times. Dividends can also pay off the original investment over a period of years. That is another reason why long term investing is a great idea to consider. By now, you should be getting the basic idea of how the Formula X rating system operates.

Just to be sure, I will take you through another list of estimated values one might assign to a stock based on its dividend yield.

Yield % = 0% = 0 −1
Yield % = .5 − 1% = 1 to 2
Yield % = 1 − 2% = 3 to 4
Yield % = 2 − 3% = 4 to 5
Yield % = 3 − 4% = 5 to 7
Yield % = 4 − 5% = 6 to 8
Yield % = 5 - 6% = 7 to 9
Yield % = 6 - 7% = 8 to 9
Yield % = 7% and above = 10

Please note, the above values are based upon the current interest rate levels while writing this book. Depending on the current interest rate level and economy, you may want to later change these values. Now that you have acquired the general idea regarding the rating system, please take the time to assign your own rating system. Use the concepts that coincide with the scale I created. Your scale does not have to match mine exactly, although it may prove easier for you to do so. You will not lose anything by giving an educated guess at your valuation if you feel comfortable with the material at hand. Once you have estimated your own stock's X rating values, compare them and see how they stack up against one another. The higher rating stocks are a better-estimated choice for growth and capital gains.

Formula X's next value used is Return on Equity. Return on Equity means 'how good a company is growing or using its earnings.' Below is a sample scale that you may adjust to suit your needs.

Indicator		Rating		Insight
ROE	=	0 – 5%	=	1
ROE	=	5 – 10%	=	2 – 3
ROE	=	11 – 13%	=	4 – 5
ROE	=	14 – 17%	=	6 – 7
ROE	=	18 – 22%	=	8
ROE	=	23 – 30%	=	9
ROE	=	>30%	=	10

I would recommend at least a 15% minimum ROE unless other factors make it attractive enough to overlook. An actual goal to look at would be above the 25% marker. This is kind of a high range to shoot for, but this factor will prove to be an important factor later for the price growth. As pointed out earlier, it is better to purchase a stock well below its book price in order to receive a better value. It is similar to buying a stock at a sale price versus at its estimated value.

Let us look at the example scale on the following page.

Indicator	Rating		Insight
Book Value =	>1.5	=	1
Book Value =	1.01 – 1.49	=	2
Book Value =	1	=	3
(Note that this is when the market price equals the book			
Book Value =	.90 - .99	=	4
Book Value =	.80 - .89	=	5
Book Value =	.70 - .79	=	6 - 7
Book Value =	.60 - .69	=	8
Book Value =	.40 - .59	=	9
Book Value =	<.39	=	10

** Make sure, for some reason, that book values are not extremely low. If the book values are low, it may indicate a company is in financial turmoil to be trading at such a low sale price. Be careful.

Indicator	Rating		Insight
Debt to Equity =	>1	=	1
Debt to Equity =	.90 - .99	=	2
Debt to Equity =	.75 - .89	=	3
Debt to Equity =	.50 - .74	=	4
Debt to Equity =	.40 - .49	=	5
Debt to Equity =	.30 - .39	=	6
Debt to Equity =	.20 - .29	=	7
Debt to Equity =	.15 - .19	=	8
Debt to Equity =	.11 - .14	=	9
Debt to Equity =	<.1	=	10

The result does not need to be a company high in debt. Once a company packs on the debt, just like an individual it is hard to get out of financial distress and it is also hard to keep the debt level as low as possible.

One of our most important ratings will be our PEG rating. As you may recall, we will be using the price to earnings ratio divided by the growth rate for the security. The lower value is the most favorable situation.

Look below at a sample scale of these values. Notice how they may be rated:

Indicator		P/E % Growth		Insight
PEG	=	>2	=	1
		(At PEG of 2, the Growth rate is equal to half the P/E)		
PEG	=	>1.5	=	2
PEG	=	1 – 1.4	=	3
		(At PEG of 1, the Growth rate is equal to the P/E)		
PEG	=	.8 - .99	=	4
PEG	=	.7 - .79	=	5
PEG	=	.6 - .69	=	6
PEG	=	.5 - .59	=	7
		(At PEG of .5 the Growth rate is 2x greater then the P/E value)		
PEG	=	.4 - .49	=	8
PEG	=	.3 - .39	=	9
PEG	=	<.29	=	10
		(At PEG of .25 the Growth rate is 4x the P/E value)		

Now look at the multiplier - the formula cannot be complete without it. It is one thing to rank only the indicators from 1 to 10. It is quite another to take into account each indicators' importance compared to the other. Each indicator has its unique value in the importance of the whole pie. Notice all the multipliers do total to a value of 1, representing 100% of the total value in the formula. Each piece of the pie is now weighed according to its value compared to the pie as a whole. Let us now determine the percentage that all the pieces of pie are worth in the equation. Use the chart below to start:

Indicator	Multiplier	Represents
P/E	.3	30%
Yield	.15	15%
ROE	.2	20%
Book Value	.05	5%
Debt to Equity	.1	10%
Growth > P/E, PEG	.2	20%
TOTAL	1	100%

By now, it should be clear that the multiplier plays an important role in the formula. Once insight rating is accounted for, you can begin to use the multipliers to give further meaning to your numbers. A clearer picture will begin to formulate in your mind as to what the values really mean. Without this process, all the indicators we have discussed so far would be weighed equally in our decision. This is not what I believe to be the case when breaking down a stock. If you like, alter the multipliers to fit your needs if you have a different opinion than I do. Just be sure to remember that all your multipliers should add up to 1, representing 100% of the pie.

Below is a visible pie chart of the weighed decision for each stock's indicators.

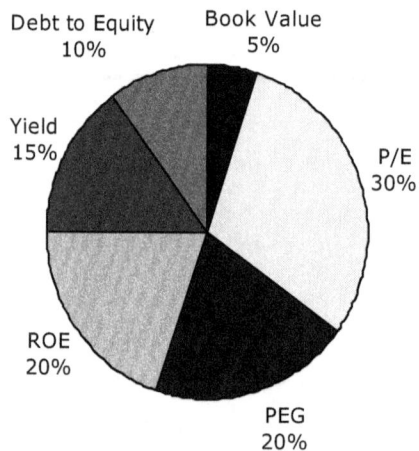

This graph shows the importance of each indicator from the least to the most important.

Now that we have finished a sample scale for all our indicators, we will finally put this to use. Let us take the previous example in the section entitled 'Example of a Security Analysis.' Notice that the calculations have already been made for the indicators, so we will plug them into our formula. Our P/E value for this stock was equal to 5. With our P/E of 5, first be sure to determine your insight rating. Then look at the sample scale of P/E values and you will see a value of 9 has been obtained for your insight rating. We may now place a 9 in Column 3 next to the P/E multiplier. Once the insight rating is obtained, multiply it by the multiplier of .3 to obtain the Formula X value of 2.7. Place this value in Column 4 under the indicator for value. However, this is not the end of your X value. In order to get the final Formula X rating; please total up the sum of your entire Formula X values (the last box in Column 4.)

EXAMPLE

INDICATOR	MULTIPLIER	INSIGHT RATING	X VALUE
P/E Value	.3	9	2.7

Now let us travel towards studying your next indicator of yield value. Previously determined was the yield value of 5% for this security. Taking a glance at this sample scale, let us obtain an estimated insight value of about 7.5. Next, place my insight rating of 7.5 into your Column 3 and multiply it by the multiplier of .15.

Following through this way will actually provide you with the X value of 1.125 in Column 4.

INDICATOR	MULTIPLIER	INSIGHT RATING	X VALUE
Yield Value	.15	7.5	1.125

Return on Equity will be the next calculation. Our example has revealed a Return on Equity of 20%. First, go again to the sample scale in order to obtain the insight rating. For this scale, an 8 seems to be suitable. Placing the 8 in Column 3 and multiplying it by a multiplier of .2 will give you an X value of 1.6. Now place a 1.6 X value in Column 4 until you obtain all the X values. Once the X values are calculated, then move on to the final step. For now, move onto the next indicator.

EXAMPLE

INDICATOR	MULTIPLIER	INSIGHT RATING	X VALUE
Return on Equity	.2	8	1.6

Book value has been previously determined to be equal to .65. Looking again at this scale, you can see that the insight rating fell on a score of 8. Next, multiply the insight rating of 8 by .05 to give you an X value of .4.

INDICATOR	MULTIPLIER	INSIGHT RATING	X VALUE
Book Value	.05	8	.4

Next, take a little more time and determine your X value for debt to equity. So far, we have established our .22 debt to equity value to lead to an insight rating of 7. Now by multiplying the two numbers, you will get an X value of .7 (7 x .1 = 7.)

EXAMPLE

INDICATOR	MULTIPLIER	INSIGHT RATING	X VALUE
Debt to Equity	.1	7	.7

Last, but not least, our last indicator, the PEG. The calculations have yielded a PEG value of .25. This is an exceptionally healthy value. As you can see from this scale, we achieve an insight rating of 10. Multiplying it by our multiplier gave us an X value of 2 (10 x .2 = 2.) If you have stuck with me and followed along without giving up, you have now completed your X values for all of the indicators.

EXAMPLE

INDICATOR	MULTIPLIER	INSIGHT RATING	X VALUE
PEG	.2	10	2

Please note that there are many other indicators that could have been added to this equation. Quick ratios and current ratios are two of the possibilities. Feel free to add indicators and multipliers once you become familiar with the material and its concepts. You may even find that other formulas are more suitable to your needs. Do not even hesitate to experiment and try a new method of security evaluation. Only by gaining more knowledge can you excel at any topic. You will find, as we gather more experience, these formulas will fall in place much easier. Try not to become overwhelmed or discouraged.

Your final picture should look like this:

INDICATOR	MULTIPLIER	INSIGHT RATING	X VALUE
P/E	.3	9	2.7
Yield	.15	7.5	1.125
ROE	.2	8	1.6
Book Value	.05	8	.4
Debt to Equity	.1	7	.7
PEG	.2	10	2
		Formula X Rating =	8.5

Finally, let us study the last process of the rating system. Let us start by adding all of the X values in Column 4 together in order to get your Formula X rating. By doing so, you obtain a value of 8.525. This value is one that is somewhat attractive for a Formula X rating. By itself, a Formula X rating will mean nothing until you compare it to another Formula X rating. Later, we will look deeper into these values by using a graph system that you can use to rank an individual security.

By studying this last process a little bit deeper, you can determine why it is so important to get a Formula X rating. You will be able to determine why you shouldn't just average out the insight rating values. Our Formula X rating will give you a more exact evaluation of your security and it will indicate why the multipliers are key there. The more important values will have a bigger weight in our rating system. Let us see exactly what the difference would be between our insight rating average and our actual Formula X rating.

Totaling up Column 3 and dividing it by 6 will give an insight rating average of 8.25 (9+7.5+8+8+7+10/6.) The difference in the numbers is .25. This number may not sound like a significant amount but it may prove to be very important in selecting a security by revealing a clearer picture later. This .25 value difference for this security could have even been to the downside instead of to the upside. What does the difference mean? When there is a situation where the difference is to the upside, as in our example, it may mean that we have some extra hidden value in the security This value is an insight rating average of 8.25 as compared to our Formula X rating of 8.5. What if the Formula X rating was to the downside of the insight rating average? The difference between the Formula X average rating and the Formula X value may mean you have over estimated the security's value. There may be something hidden. The majority of the more important indicators may actually be lagging some as compared to the least important indicators.

If at this time you can tell your formula is not accurate, establish a range of numbers that you could estimate to be the value of your security. The insight rating average was 8.25 with a difference of .25 between it and the true Formula X rating value. You know that this range is in favor of the upside due to our calculations; however, you could give an estimated range of 8.25 + .25 = 8 - 8.5. This would be a more conservative range value for the security. The least conservative range would be taking the Formula X rating and granting that a range of +/- .25. Now an overrated range may exist of 8.25 – 8.75. For our purposes, this security may seem to have some hidden value in it because the rating is to the upside. Hidden values between the average and the X rating seem more attractive when the X rating is above the insight rating average. This may help sway your decision between two securities with similar ratings. The main goal at this time is to allow us to achieve a method, which will make comparisons. We want the decision to pop out at us!

Your first Formula X rating for a security is established. Let us compare it to another stock and see possible ranges that may develop in our analysis. Begin by comparing one security to another security in the technology sector.

The calculated values of the two securities are below for your convenience. Once you have completed this exercise, use the provided formula and compare your results to mine.

P/E	=	36
Yield	=	1%
ROE	=	15%
Book Value	=	1.6
Debt to Equity	=	.9
PEG	=	.8

By doing your calculations you should of come up with a value of 4.15 for your X rating. Check your work below:

INDICATOR	MULTIPLIER	INSIGHT RATING	X VALUE
P/E	.3	4.5	1.35
Yield	.15	3	.45
ROE	.2	6.5	1.3
Book Value	.05	1	.05
Debt to Equity	.1	2	.2
PEG	.2	4	.8
		X Rating =	4.15

106

From the two security evaluations we have drawn, the conclusion is that the first security is much more attractive in the sense of value. However, this does not mean that our conclusion will always remain the same. It is important to keep track of both these securities on a graph to determine which way they are heading. Keeping track on a weekly, monthly, quarterly or even biannual basis is a great idea. This method is good to use if you have not yet purchased a security in that it will give you an idea of future levels of attractiveness. Once the market price for the first security rises, the stock may fall lower down the attractiveness scale. This is mainly due to an increase in the P/E ratio as the market price rises. It is also possible that the EPS will not be the same as in recent months. Many things can change over time. Earning warnings can cut the price of a security drastically, depending on the severity of the call. Nevertheless, we must do all we can on our part to track the security.

The Formula X system may also benefit us in determining when we should sell out of a winning position. If our Formula X rating falls to a certain level, it may send us a signal to sell. If our rating is increasing with a security we have in our portfolio, we may want to hold onto the stock a little longer. This will allow the market to recognize its value. The main goal is to give you a better feeling on where your security might be heading.

I have devised a simple diagram below to illustrate a general ranking for different X ratings.

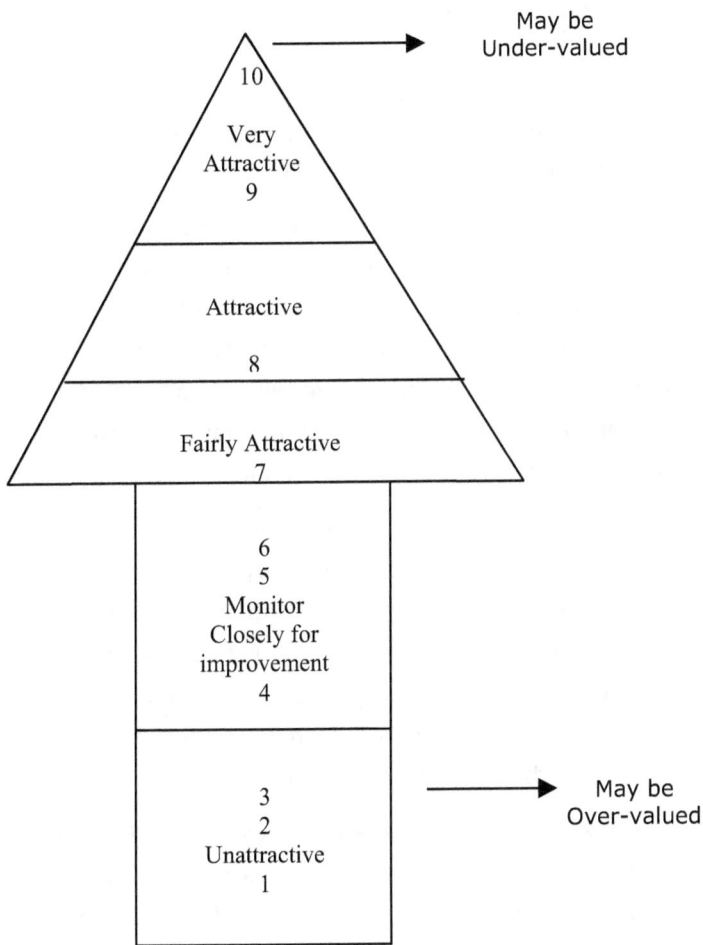

CHAPTER 17:

COMPANY 'X' RATING VALUE OVER TIME

Once you establish an 'X' value rating for a stock, you will be able to develop a method to chart the progress of the stock.

Take all of the company names that you have begun to look at in a particular sector. Create a list with all of these company names. Continue comparing the companies. Next, assign each one their 'X' value. At this point, begin to fill in the appropriate box in the following chart for each stock. I promise you that this rating system will end up being of real value to you. This chart can become the great indicator for you to study in order to see if a company is progressing or losing ground compared to its peers.

I would suggest that you, every few months, take a bit more time to re-evaluate the ratings for each company. By doing this, you can stay on top of the fluctuating changes in the marketplace and begin to learn if the fundamentals are growing stronger. This will help you to determine if an over-achieving company is starting to fall off in the group you have put together. You will also begin to see if an underachieving company is working its way up to the top of the mountain.

In the following chart, there are two columns indicating current ranking and previous ranking. These columns determine the rise or fall on the sector ladder of a particular stock. With this rating system, you will be able to avoid buying the stocks you see are at the top of the sector that appear to be heading downwards. Fill out each area of the chart. Then take the time to study the chart knowing it will help you filter out undervalued stocks rising to the top of its sector. Please take note, time intervals may vary depending on your preference.

SECTOR=_____

Previous Ranking	Current Ranking	Company	Jan	Feb	Mar	Apr	May	June	July	Aug	Sept	Oct	Nov	Dec

SECTOR=_____

Previous Ranking	Current Ranking	Company	Jan	Feb	Mar	Apr	May	June	July	Aug	Sept	Oct	Nov	Dec

CHAPTER 18

THE COMPARISON LIST

The charts in the previous chapter can prove to be very helpful while learning the Formula X system. Through these charts it will become easier for you to compare the Formula X values over a specific time. Many parameters can be compared that will be helpful to you. One such parameter not yet studied is a company's income revenue over time. Revenue increases and decreases over time can help in determining whether business is improving or losing steam. When there is a recession, chances are that revenues will drop. Some people believe that when the economy is 'rolling on all fours,' revenues should be increasing quarter after quarter. A great leap in revenues, quarter after quarter, might cause a company to make more profits than it did the last quarter. However, this may not always be the case. It is suggested profit margins contained in these excess revenues always be taken into consideration.

If profit margins are cut drastically from the previous quarter, it is possible to find out you may have actually made more profits the quarter before. This can happen, although revenues may have increased slightly higher than they had been in the past. A wise decision would be to search for a drop in revenues to be a sign of decreasing fundamentals. One might be able to surmise that something could actually be going wrong.

If something appears to be wrong (the stock price is dropping substantially fast), ask yourself a couple of questions. Could the decreasing fundamentals be due to a slow down in the economy? Does it appear that something is wrong because a company is losing its market share to another competitor in the same sector? By keeping records of increases and decreases in the revenues across a sector, you will be able to acquire knowledge about which company is actually gaining ground on their competitors. The competitor losing ground can be noticed as well. By taking the time to rank the companies according to their revenues, you will vividly get an idea about which company is moving up the ladder. Make sure you then take even more time to rank which company is taking a fall down the ladder.

Usually when a company reports earnings, you will see revenue changes stated and you will be able to compare the earnings to a previous quarter. Revenue increases or decreases in a stock may have an affect on the sentiment and the price of the stock. 'Earnings per share' is also the main number that companies report along with their revenue changes. Of course, a company usually is trying to beat 'estimated earnings.' By falling in line or beating these estimated earnings, the produced data will show that a company is on track. This data will also provide you the knowledge of where the company should be at any given time. Falling below estimates can prove to be detrimental to a company's stock price as well as fundamental stability.

Wall Street sometimes tends to buy on rumor and sell on fact. Ever wonder why a company reports its earnings and then either rises or falls substantially shortly afterwards? Some companies manage to fall perfectly in line with estimates but then they tumble. The reason why this happens is that stock price volatility may be higher than usual during periods of earning forecasts.

Management teams can play a significant role in a company's future progress to the up or down side. A well experienced team can find new paths of obtaining new business prospects or by obtaining new products. Some may under-go a new restructuring program in order to cut costs. This acquired data should also be placed on your list to help you to compare the different stocks.

If you were in a car race, who would you want to be at the wheel? A seasoned veteran race car driver or a rookie driver that is racing in his first start? The answer to this question is easy. You would choose a seasoned driver. In the same sense, this book will (if studied and then applied) will cause you to become a seasoned and successful stock trader. The above parameter is just one example of what you should study. Now that you are learning, surely you can come up with other parameters to compare securities. By all means, please use your own insights and chart them on a ranking system.

Below is a sample list of parameters that may help you as you begin to travel your road to success.

1.   Revenues
2.   Management Team
3.   Earnings Per Share
4.   P/E Value
5.   P/S Value
6.   PEG
7.   Profit Margin
8.   Yield
9.   Return On Equity
10. Book Value
11. Debt to Equity
12. Growth Rate
13. Formula "X" Values
14. Insider Buying
15. Upgrades or Downgrades

The management team needs to be mentioned to effectively teach Formula X. The truth is, without an efficient team at the helm of things, a company's stock price may not reach its full potential. To make a decision if the company you have picked has a good management team, please ask yourself the following questions. Is the company's profits being used wisely? Is the company making good or bad judgments on mergers or acquisitions? Is the company over or under expanding? Is enough money going back into the company for research and development?

All of the above comments and questions are good data to study, however, the last question was very important. In order for a company to be number one or to maintain top status in years to come, it must be on top of its' game. Officials (management team) running the company should be experienced and have a fine track record of past accomplishments.

**Even the best company, if it ends up having the worst management team, can drive itself to the ground. You will find once you begin to use the Formula X system, you may be able to spot a bad company. Keep in mind, it is possible for a company placed out of favor to obtain a new management team and turn things around. Watching for companies to come back can be part of your study also. This may serve as a catalyst for a recovery due to new business adventures, job cuts and restructuring.

What in general drives up stock prices? To the value investor, the answer should be earnings at a fair price. Without earnings, a company should not be in business. Many of the so-called high flyer Internet stocks have had negative earnings throughout their history. Many of these companies have stated that they will not have positive earnings for a couple of years. Funny, but here it is a couple of years later and some of those companies no longer exist. Most of those companies took the route of advertising all their money and profits toward future returns. Some companies spent money on great advertising, but too much advertising not helping a bottom line can send a company to bankruptcy. To the very bottom of the barrel!

The best company to place your hard-earned cash in is one that, over time, has consistent earnings. An increase in earnings over many years can prove that the company has been growing each year. Another point to make would be for you to invest in a company that can sustain these earnings in the future. This book teaches you how to spot which companies that might actually end up being. You may even want to track a stock's history in times of hardship and see how the stock performed. EARNINGS, EARNINGS and EARNINGS are the three things that drive up stock prices!

Value investing parameters will play important roles in the selection process. As we have already covered these under the value investing section, we will not go into much detail with them again. One thought though is for you to make sure the indicator ranges all fall in line with normal attractive levels. Make sure that no danger signals exist with any of them. If you are uncomfortable with the parameters of a stock, chances are the stock might not be the one for you to purchase. Many of the parameters such as P/E, P/S, ROE, PEG, book value, debt to equity and beta values can be found using an Internet service.

There are also publications coming out on a monthly or quarterly basis that update these parameters of a stock as they change. A wise choice would be to subscribe to one of these services. Having this knowledge will save you time (and ultimately money) on the calculations. The publications also provide an abundant source for other information. Please be aware of the fact that information changes constantly. Therefore, from time to time, decide whether to use older statistics or exact current numbers.

How can you earn money on your investment when the economy is bad and the stocks you have picked have fallen? In this scenario, a person might be looking at a stock with a high yield percentage. How do your investments yield you back money even if you have badly beaten stocks in your portfolio? The answer is, in the dividend. You can also analyze what a company does when they make money. Management teams divide the money and use the money in many different areas. Some of the money is spent on advertising, employees need to be paid, research and development has to continue, acquisitions need to be settled, and an investment opportunity could still be knocking at their door. All avenues need to be taken into consideration by the team.

Let us try to look at dividends in the same way that we looked at the company's earnings. Even more money may go back to shareholders in a dividend. A dividend is a kind of a kickback for owning and holding onto company shares. One truth is that you will want to buy stock in a company that has an increasing dividend over many years. What you do not want to find is decreasing dividends or even periods where there were no dividends paid out at all. You must also keep in mind that just because your stock price is yielding 7% now, this does not mean that this value will not fall down or even cease altogether. Companies can cut and increase their dividends when they feel it appropriate to do so. These dividends may often provide a means of income throughout bad times in the market. Income investors use dividends as a driving force in their buying and selling decisions. My goal is to have a high yielding security just in case the market plummets. I have found sometimes that I have made a miscalculation in the future of the stock I have picked. So try to stay on top of your analyzing and pick a high yielding stock.

Insider buying and selling is another item that demands attention. Besides, who knows the company better than the insiders do? From time to time, officials sell some stock to pay bills, need money for vacations, or maybe even for emergency reasons. Nevertheless, for the most part, I would say that insiders have smart money. Caution -- it may not be a wise decision to buy company stock when the CEO, Vice-President and/or the majority of its' officials are selling their stocks and heading for the hills. This might have been a drastic example, but the point needs to be made clear. Buy when the insiders buy, sell when they sell.

Stock buy-backs are also an indication of an entry point into a stock. When this happens, the company feels confident about its stock at that current price level. The company wants to buy back their stock at a cheaper price expecting the stock price to go upward somewhere in the near future. Take note, a company does not have to buy back all of its shares that it stated it would. The majority of companies do fall short of completing the entire buy-back process.

If you are using technical analysis, then the wise decision might be to place a star on the points while you chart when you notice insider buying or selling has occurred. Use the same manner to plot upgrades

118

and downgrades. These circumstances can cause drastic price movements of the stock you have chosen to buy.

Before purchasing a stock, study the market capitalization. Find out if you will be getting into a huge company with plenty of cash flow and monetary reserve. This may be a very favorable position. Sometimes companies have very small market capitalizations and may not have the funds to endure a recession. Avoid trading stocks that are bought and sold, known as pink sheet stocks. These may have small market capitalizations due to small numbers of circulated shares. With these stocks, the volume is very low and it may be hard to get rid of unwanted shares.

The future of many companies lies within their product pipelines. They may have excellent products at the current times. However, what will happen when their products get outdated? If a product produces well now, who is to say that it will produce well three years from now? Research and development helps to create more of these products in order to sustain growth over the years to come. Research and development is very popular in the pharmaceutical industry.

Let us say a company comes out with a blockbuster medication and then gains a fortune for the company. Ten years pass and their patent rights expire. As soon as the patent rights expire, twenty or more generic companies scurry to produce the same product but at a cheaper price. They begin to pour the new products into the market. The once blockbuster medication has now fallen in sales drastically. Without a product pipeline, this company will soon deteriorate and future growth will actually stunt. A better managed company who has a research and development department, may come out with a new blockbuster at the end of the ten-year period. This new blockbuster will ensure future sales and revenue growth and in turn, allow the company to stay afloat.

Competition exists in almost every industry. Competition is always waiting in the wings to flood the market. Before purchasing a stock, I suggest you scout out the competition that applies in the sectors you have chosen. Find out if the company you have picked is the leader in its sector? Is the company losing ground? Is the company passing up the competition? Is the price range of their products competitive and lower than the rest? There are unlimited possibilities to look for and to learn while you become familiar with the proven method of Formula X.

One of the biggest breaks a company can come up with is a new product or a new technology. New products or a new technology could actually be something that has not yet existed in the past for any company. Therefore, the opportunity to make money at the time might appear endless. However, it is very important to be careful. These new products or new technology stocks are usually the stocks that are trading at a higher multiple due to future expectations. New technologies can also cut down the current costs of operations or expand its customer base throughout the world. These are just some concepts to keep in mind when exploring business opportunities. You may wish to add more to my list as you feel appropriate and as you learn the Formula X method.

CHAPTER 19:
TECHNICAL ANALYSIS

So far, the information presented in the preceding chapters allows you, as a stock trader, to go deeper into the fundamental analysis of a company. Now, it is time for us to go even one more step further into studying a company's stock. The next information to study is the technical analysis of the company's stock price chart patterns. My stock trading experience has taught me that fundamental and technical analysis are of the utmost importance.

To be successful at trading stocks, the idea is to learn to invest in a growing, stable company with a bright outlook. Technical analysis is available for you to use as a tool to aid you in the analysis of the charts once you have finished studying this book. Remember to first learn the fundamentals and than learn the technical aspects of trading.

In regards to the technical aspects of trading, you will learn how to analyze a company's stock so that you will be able to determine when a company starts to make its move to the upside. Many undervalued bargain companies make moves to the upside once discovered.

Some of these technical analysis concepts will not matter much due to our long term investment strategy, but it may provide us with valuable information as to when or where we should make our entry point into a stock. Value investing should not really be based on these concepts due to the long-term investment strategy. However, it will help you to move your money into an undervalued stock that is considered on the move rather than stagnant.

Many day traders of modern times use these methods of technical analysis on a daily basis in order to spot out momentum plays in the market. We will look at this method of technical analysis as an indicator of price breakout points over a long period for our securities. Day traders use daily charts consistently throughout the day from the opening bell to the close of the market. Their charts are all updated in real time allowing them to make spur of the moment decisions on their trades. By the time you understand and are able to analyze, in a technical way, a company's stock, you will be able to use weekly, monthly and even yearly graphs.

Have you ever heard the popular term 'the trend is our friend?' Catching an early trend and riding it to the top may establish outstanding capital gains.

One of the main purposes for learning to use technical analysis of a stock is so that your money will not be left parked in an unnoticed security. In order for gains to come, you need buyers. Buyers cause share prices to rise to new levels. Stocks do not rise, for the most part, substantially over night. Nor do stock prices rise straight to the top right away. Just as Rome was not built in one day, nor is a security's stock price. If you learn to locate the right stock, consistent gains will come in the long term.

Now let us talk about an example of a company that trades sideways. This type of stock is one that has fallen into a consistent pattern of going nowhere; and, it usually has a narrow range of trading. A stock trading sideways goes up a few points or less and then the stock price goes back down a couple of points or even less. This type of stock trades in a 'narrow trading range' and usually shows no gains that can be kept for any length of time.

For example, let us say you have held onto a particular stock for as long as a year. At the end of that year, some attention should be paid to a couple of negative aspects. One negative aspect would be if you were to find out that the company does not pay dividends. Investigate before hand to see if a company pays dividends. If you do research first, you will not have to have this negative aspect be a part of your experience. Another negative piece of information you could learn about your investment would be if it has low yields or not. Both of these facts show that the invested money would not actually be working to its full potential. At the end of the year, you might still have your initial investment. Even so, a savings account could have even been a better investment than an investment with negative parameters such as these. Note, an income stock may provide funds over time even when it does trade sideways. The following is an example of a company trading in a 'sideways' manner.

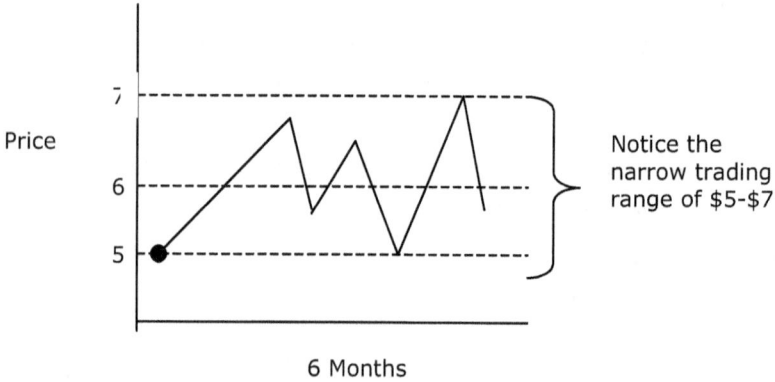

By observing the above chart, you will be able to realize that this company's stock has not grown. Over a long time, the stock price finally came back to the original five-dollar investment value. If, however, you had invested in aggressive growth stock companies who paid out no dividends over a prolonged period, you would have had zero capital gains. If you had invested in a company such as Phillip Morris, they may have given you decent returns. Phillip Morris has a history of high yields being made in that same amount of time (check yields due to the constant change in the market.)

Another type of stock movement is one that climbs to higher levels consistently. Some stocks have a balanced trend. Some stocks, on the other hand, have an upward trend. As mentioned earlier, usually a straight-line movement is not normal. A jagged flow usually shows that the stock rises and lowers at different points. The observation of higher highs and lower lows begins to develop. The ladder at the top begins to take shape and a pattern forms. Look at the chart below and take the time to study it. This is the exact information needed in order to obtain a technical analysis from a stock pattern. This trend is one that is important. Missing this point could be detrimental to your success.

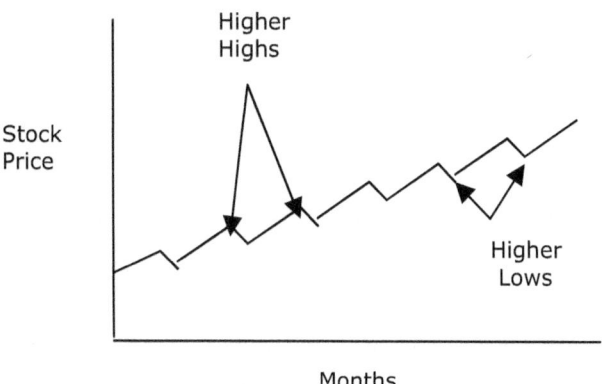

Unless there is a crucial and significant sign of a turn around, avoid unfavorable trends. If you can tell that the stock you want to invest in is in a declining trend, and that the stock shows no real sign of stabilizing or achieving a support level, then avoid it. If no support level can be achieved then no base price will be established. A slow and constant nosedive is destined to come. The characterization of this trend is one of a stock trading at successive points of lower highs and lower lows. Be careful to learn the three patterns discussed so far in order to be able to spot them out easily.

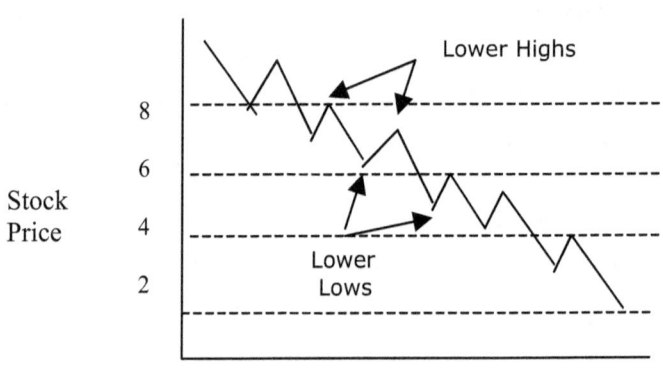

Months

Now that you have studied this book and learned a great deal about trading, I would like you to see if you are able to notice a pattern that has developed in both of these charts. In our previous example of an upward trend, we developed a 2:1 ratio of incline versus decline (two up for one down.) This current example, shows the same ratio of 2:1 (two down for one up,) which is an unfavorable situation unless the security is shorted of course.

So far, we have seen a sideways, an upward and a downward trend. The motive of the technical analysis is to be able to determine when you believe these patterns will perform a reversal or breakout of its normal trading range. This is a 'stock breakout,' 'breakaway,' or 'reversal point.' Further analyzing the stock patterns, you will learn to determine when a stock initially breaks out of its normal trading range. Once a stock breaks out of its normal trading range, you may find a substantial burst to the upside or downside. Bases in stocks are formed by investors' support levels while peaks are formed by resistance levels or selling pressures in a stock. A very important breakout to spot is a stock trading sideways for a long amount of time. This pattern starts to show its deviation from its normal trading range. Take a moment now and draw a line across the chart. Locate the intercepting point called the 'crossing point.' In an upward breakout our crossing point will be our entry point whereas in a downward trend, our crossing point will be our selling point.

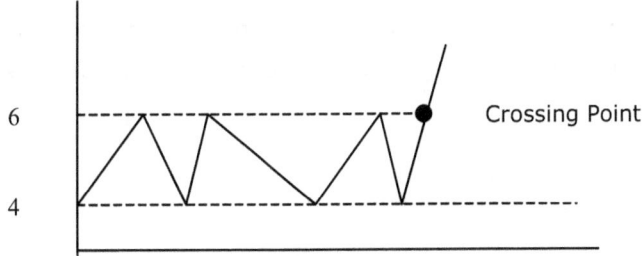

Our trading range is $4 - $6 for a long amount of time. Suddenly the stock breaks out of its cycle going to the upside. The stock reaches beyond its $6 market price. The resistance point (where sellers exit) has been overcome and there is no telling how high this stock may now rise.

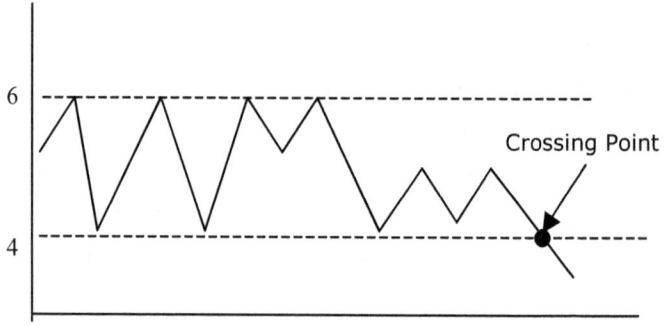

Support levels have been broken, BAIL OUT! This stock actually broke out below its $4 support level. These are the simpler examples that exist that use the same concept of trading ranges. They use a dividing line to find crossing points so you can develop skills in more complex charting situations. This information is for beginners, not professionals. This book is helpful with the concepts and ideas behind technical analysis.

The following examples are of a couple of other basic charts.

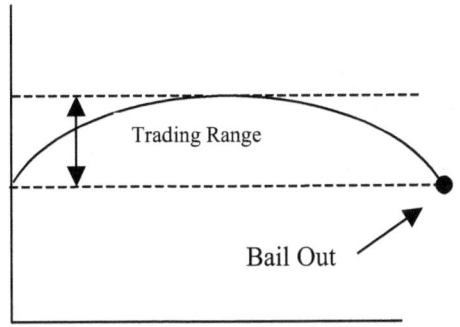

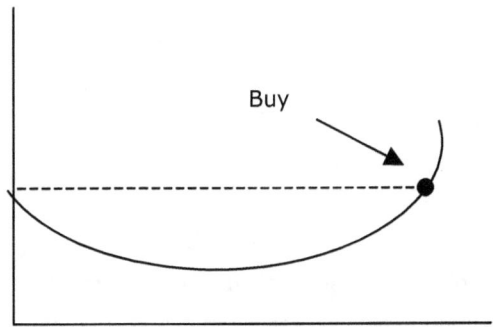

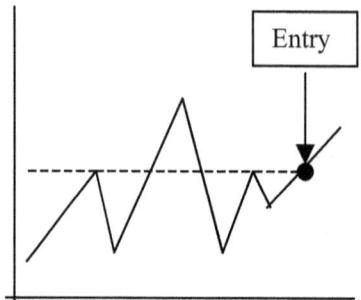

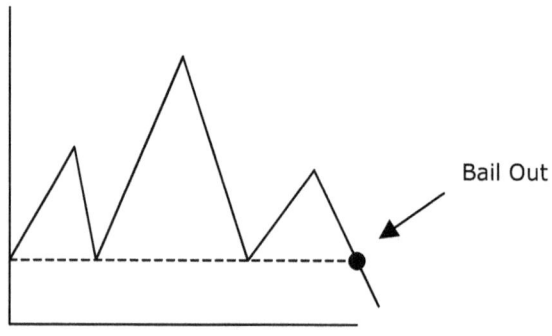

These sell-off points are just ideas to provide you with information on when not to enter a long stock position. In a bad economic downturn, the positive and successful goal is to hold onto your stocks for the long term by using fundamental analysis. Technical analysis may help you to avoid buying stocks at breakout points to the downside. Try your utmost to grasp as many concepts as possible before making any buying or selling decisions.

CHAPTER 20:
TYPES OF ORDERS

You will learn several types of orders in this chapter. The more you learn about orders, the better a trader you will become. Market orders are the most popular order. A market order is an order to buy or sell at the best current available price according to the best bid or best offer price. Market orders can serve just as well when investing for the long term. Take note, when market orders are used, the price may be a slight bit higher.

Another type of order is a 'limit order.' The majority of the nation's public does not even know about this type of order. Day traders all around the world make their living using limit orders throughout the day (referred to as teenie traders.) When investing for the long term in undervalued stocks it is not as important to try to use limit orders.

For every stock, there is a spread. The spread makes up the best bid and the best offer price at that time. Traders sometimes try to manipulate the spread by using limit orders in order to cut the spread down lower, therefore maximizing profits. In a large spread security, costs can be cut down substantially by using limit orders when purchasing a large quantity of shares. Here is an example of stock 'ABCD' and what information about the stock may appear like on an online broker screen.

$10 (bid) - $10 ¼ (ask)

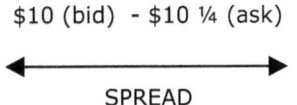

SPREAD

Note: Decimalization has changed the quote to $10 - $10.25

By looking at the example, you can tell that this stock is trading at $10 to $10-1/4. Notice the stock bid price is $10. Look further and you will find that the stock has an ask price of $10-1/4. To help you further understand, let us just say the 'bid price' is the highest current price in which a trader is willing to pay for the stock. 'Ask price' is the least amount of money that the trader will accept from a bidder at bid time. In this example, when buying at the market price, you will be purchasing shares at the ask price of $10-1/4. When you sell shares at the market price, you will receive a price of $10. This is the highest bid price at the time of the bid.

The spread in the stock 'ABCD' is 1/4 of a point (the difference between the 'ask price' and the 'bid price'.) As earlier stated, a day trader may attempt using a limit order to cut the spread down some. A limit order is an order that states the price is being limited to what you will pay for a stock. Day traders usually place a limit order between the spread at about maybe $10-1/16. Instead of purchasing shares at the market price of $10-1/4, they will try to purchase them at $10-1/16 and turn them over again at $10-1/8. Observe the following process:

$10 (bid) - $10.25 (ask)

Becomes

$10.0625 - $10.25 (new limit)

Becomes

$10 (old bid) - $10.125 (new limit order to sell shares)

Notice how the new bid now becomes the day trader's bid at $10.0625. The trader currently has the highest buying price or bid in the market. This bid will execute first on another trader's market order to sell. If our day trader purchases his shares at $10.0625 and nobody else is on that same purchase price, the bid should drop back to its original $10 bid ($10-10.25.) Now that the trader purchased the shares at $10.0625, the spread goes back to its original position.

$$\$10 - \$10.25$$

The trader now wishes to sell the purchased shares off for a small profit at $10.1875. Therefore, the trader cuts the spread again and places a sell limit order at 10.1875. The new spread becomes:

$$\$10 - \$10.1875$$

Once his shares disappear, the spread jumps back to its original position as long as no new orders come into the market.

$$\$10 - \$10.25$$

If a trader already owns these shares and wants to sell them at a higher price than $10, the trader can place a sale limit order above the current bid price of $10.25. Let us say, for example, the trader wanted to sell the purchased shares for $10.1875. What the trader would do is to place a sale limit order to sell at $10.1875 and the new equation would become:

$$\$10 - \$10.25$$
$$\$10 - \$10.1875 \text{ (his sell limit order)}$$

Currently this trader has the best selling price and it will show up as the best price advertised across ticker tape screens. If a market order to buy shares were to present itself now, the seller with this lower ask price of $10.1875 would sell his shares before anyone else and the sale would execute. Once the shares are sold, the spread would become its original $10 to $10.25. Sounds simple, right? Let us take this lesson one step further. Two more facts you must take into consideration are timing and volume. Also of importance is knowing where you are in line to do your purchasing or selling. Let us now place the volume of the share.

$10 (bid price) - $10.125 (ask price)
50 (bid size)   20   (ask size)

The bid size and ask size tell a trader how many shares can be bought and/or sold at that particular price level. Depending on what service the trader is using, a trader might see only the inside bid, ask price and size. Other bid and ask prices may appear if a person were trading on a more upgraded version of trading. Day traders due to their advantage in information more commonly use NASDAQ, with level two screens. Bid size and ask size are portrayed in lots of 100's. In other words, 10 points would represent 1000 shares. In our example above 5000 shares (50 x 100) are willing to be bought at the bid price of $10 while 2000 shares (20 x 100) are willing to be sold at $10.125.

Looking at the current example (at this time,) the majority of the shares seem like they want to be bought when the inside bid size is compared to the inside ask size. Be sure to realize that other unseen orders do exist. These orders can shift the stock's price or momentum drastically. We are comparing the current price of the stocks at that

133

instant in time. Bid and ask sizes can give you a hint to momentum swings at times when a huge order comes into the market that can cause an imbalance in supply and demand. It is imperative, if you are going to be a successful trader, for you to think of this as a game. At this point in the study of this book, it is imperative for you to try to understand what is happening when all four of these numbers change (bid + ask prices, bid + ask sizes.)

Using the diagram mentioned previously, think about buying 2000 shares at 10.0625 and look what this becomes:

$$\$10.0625 \ - \ \$10.125$$
$$20 \qquad\qquad 20$$

The bid size of 20 represents your 2000 shares at the bid price of $10.0625.

Say you wanted to buy 2000 shares and to do so, you wanted to place a limit order on the bid price of $10. This now becomes:

$$\$10 \ - \ \$10.125$$
$$70 \qquad\qquad 20$$

The spread stays the same because you did not alter the prices in any way. However, let us look at the fact that the bid size went up from 50 or 5000 shares; and then up again to 70 or 7000 shares to take into account your order for an additional 2000 shares (7000-5000=2000.)

Now, let us say you wanted to sell the 2000 shares and place a limit order on the ask price of $10.125. This action would look like:

$10 (bid price) - $10.125 (ask price)

50 (bid size)   40   (ask size)

Your ask price size has suddenly increased by 20 taking into account your additional order for the 2000 shares.

Suppose we change the order for a minute to be that you wanted to sell 2000 shares at the market price. This action now becomes:

$10 (bid size) - $10.125 (ask price)

30 (bid size)   20   (ask size)

What do you believe happened here? When you sell shares at the market price, people who are on the highest inside bid will buy them. So when you sell 2000 shares (20) you must deduct that number from the buyer's or the bid size. Initially 5000 shares were asking for a bid of $10. Now that you sold those 2000 shares, only 3000 shares are waiting to be purchased; henceforth, the 30 bid size value.

Now, let us place an order to buy of 1000 shares at the market price. This action becomes:

$10 (bid size) - $10.125 (ask price)

50 (bid size)   10   (ask size)

In this example, the ask size is what is affected. When market orders are placed, traders buy at the ask price and sell at the bid price. When traders buy the 1000 shares at the market at the ask price, the ask size drops from 20 to 10. Originally, 2000 shares were waiting for a bid at that price. Now with the purchase of 1000 shares, only 1000 more are waiting to be sold at that price.

A great thing to do is just sit back at your computer and observe a stock trading at a low to moderate daily volume. Seriously, study the stock carefully throughout the day. Learn how to observe the bid and ask prices. Notice all bid size changes and draw some conclusions of your own as to why the changes occurred. With each trade, you should learn to understand what is happening to the stocks. Try to picture trading and studying stock trading as a game. Play detective deciphering what the number changes mean in your head. The more you do this, the more familiar you will become with this concept.

Try to learn the information below by studying how price movements fluctuate depending upon the size of the orders. Sometimes it is possible to place one order and have that order fill at two different prices depending upon the size of shares traded at a specific time. Depending on what service you are using, you may or may not have this information available to you. Long-term investors learn enough that they do not even need to know the information before and after the inside bid and ask. Time will show all of the shares' true value and a daily or intra-day momentum swing will not mean much to us in the end.

Bids:	$9.875	$10	-	$10.125	$10.25	(asks)
Sizes:	50	50		20	50	(sizes)

Volume: 50,000 shares traded so far for the day

In these market conditions, let us place an order to buy 6000 shares at the market price. What happens when only 2000 shares are on the particular asking price? Answer, a price jump or up-tick occurs for the stock. The 2000 shares will be soaked up by our market order and the price will jump to $10.25. We still have 4000 shares to buy. These shares then deduct from the number of shares at the $10.25 price. The 5000 shares there will act as a sponge and soak up our remaining order. We will subtract our 4000 shares from the 5000 share size waiting to be sold at $10.25. This will leave 1000 shares remaining on that stock price level. With this order, we have purchased 2000 shares at $10.125 and 4000 shares at $10.25 to complete our order. The new spread quickly becomes the following:

$10 - $10.25

50   10

Volume: 56,000

This spread will not remain this wide for very long. When new buyers or new sellers come into the market, the spread will change. The spread is currently .25 in this circumstance. In reality, a spread this wide might not be found too often unless you are dealing with a stock which is not well known or has low trading volume. It is important to buy stocks with high trading volumes, unless you are a day trader that likes to seek out low volume stocks with greater spreads in order to manipulate.

Whenever a trade is finished, the trade will appear in its volume for the day. So far, in the example above, we had a volume of 50,000 shares for the day before we made our trade. Once our trade registers, the daily volume accounts for the share purchase of 6,000 and becomes 56,000.

Volume is a very important tool to use when dealing with a stock that has low volume. This tool is also important to use when a stock specialist or market maker is in the market for your stock. Sometimes they can refresh bids or ask sizes before you even know a trade happens. The volume indicator will always keep you aware of any shares traded.

Not knowing any information past the inside bid or ask bid and not taking into account whether or not a big seller or buyer will come into the market, we will guess where the stock will be heading. Of course, all the factors just mentioned would swing momentum differently, so be careful.

Inside Bid, Inside Ask

$10 (bid) – $10.125 (ask)

300 (bid size)   50 (ask size)

Momentum Trend (with no other outside factors)

$10 (bid price) – $10.125 (ask price)

50 (bid size)   300 (ask size)

Momentum Trend (with no other outside factors)

$9.875	$10 – $10.125	$10.1875
1000	300 – 50	10

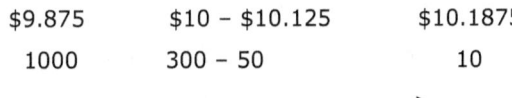

Momentum Trend (with no other outside factors)

$9.875	$10 – $10.125	$10.1875
3000	20 – 200	50

◄───────────────────────────

Short Term Shift (may be negative)

───────────────────────────►

Long Term Shift (may be positive)

This is a very strong support level at $9.875. Chances are this price level will hold unless a bigger seller comes in. If you were to buy this stock at $9.875, you would have a stable support level for the moment, all things not changing.

Important Point:

$10 - $10.125
50   50

If you place an order to buy 1,000 shares of this stock as a limit order on the bid price of $10 the new scenario will be:

$10 – $10.125   10 = yours
60 -   50   50 = theirs

In order to sell your shares, the 50 or 5,000 shares placed in front of your order must first be purchased from sellers before your order executes. It is all about who gets to the position first. This is what determines when your order fills.

If this topic interests you, obtain more literature on the subject and learn more. Again, our main goal is to invest for the long-term and be value investors. These short-term investment movements should not affect traders who learn how to trade using the Formula X method at all long-term.

Another important order besides market and limit orders is the 'stop loss order.' A 'stop order loss' is usually placed below your price to reduce your downside risk. For example, let us say you purchased a stock at $20. You are sure you cannot afford it to drop to $15 or $16. Once the stock's price hits your stop order price, your order becomes a market order. The order actually executes at the next best price at the time. Other orders do exist. For the purposes of learning the Formula X method, market orders are fine when value investing.

CHAPTER 21:
MOMENTUM PLAYS

Day traders play the market based on their hunches of market swings. They also base some of their buys upon stock price momentum and/or breaking news. The Dow, NASDAQ, and S + P futures are good indicators on how the market will perform when the opening bell rings. There are three indexes to monitor when entering a short-term trade.

Take the time to consider market breadth before entering daily trades. Market breadth is the measure of advancing stocks versus declining stocks. It may be a little riskier to enter a long position when more declining stocks are evident than advancing stocks in a high ratio. The reverse also applies when taking a short position in a positive market breadth situation.

Interest rate changes are another factor that day traders study. They use them in order to try to gain profits on a pop in stock prices. This strategy is very risky. Sometimes even when rates get cut, the market might still fall or actually even go up for that matter. Interest rate hikes usually make the public and the street talk and changes are expected.

Earnings may also be a spotlight for some traders. When companies beat earnings expectations with an increase in revenues, chances are the stock will trade upward or gap upward when reports come out after the bell. When a company lowers its outlooks or estimates, the opposite can also occur. The stock market is very mysterious. More often than not, unexpected turns occur when you believe the opposite will happen. The market has dwindled away many a day traders' capital over the years.

Value investing should be of utmost priority when you do your homework and are trying to determine strategies for the future. Analyst's upgrades and downgrades can also make or break a stock depending upon the reputation of the analysts or the companies. An upgrade can bolster a stock price by raising its future expectations or optimism about a stock. Sometimes a downgrade can devastate a stock by half or even more. Day traders must confront many challenges in trying to limit their downside loss and risk potential. Successful stock trading is a game of patience, skill, and risk management. Before entering a trade, a profit and maximum loss mark should already be set in place. Establish in your mind beforehand a price limit on gains and losses both.

A war or natural devastation can affect stock prices. One of the changes most likely to occur after a war begins is that certain surpluses are bought and sold more afterwards than before the war. A real vivid example would be that of the buying and selling of airplanes. Once the purchase and sale has transpired and signed contracts are in hand with purchase orders fulfilled, many different companies will become more quickly successful. Another example might be that if there are a lot of injuries and a lot of medical supplies are bought and sold, then those companies supplying the medical equipment become more successful quickly. These might be stocks to watch. Once a natural devastation such as a tropical storm or hurricane hits a city or area, certain goods and/or surpluses are used more than before the storm. Companies that may have been very successful before a natural disaster may be struck by a hurricane one day and have no way to open shop the next day. This would surely cause the company to have financial problems if not put them in bankruptcy altogether. Therefore in all of these situations, stocks may rise or fall depending upon the certainty or level of the successes and damages caused by the wars or natural disasters.

Momentum in stocks can increase when a CEO of a company, as a guest on a television broadcast, says and does all the right things in the public's viewpoint. An unsuccessful interview of a President or Vice President of the nation can also cause momentum in securities to change. In essence, stock prices of any market, on any day, can reflect positive and/or negative trends depending upon the nature of the news.

Positions taken while using day trading strategies usually close out before the end of the day. Many things can happen after the bell rings to end a trading session. On bad news, a stock may gap down substantially before you can get out of your position. Proceed with strict caution if you decide to take this trading route. Getting out when stocks are going down is not always the best decision you can make.

When great news about a company comes out before the end of trading day, the price usually gets gapped upward early at the 9:30 a.m. bell. I have noticed that market orders placed before the opening of the markets are usually executed at the high for the day although this may not always be the case. However, it is possible for the security to rally to higher levels after subsequent news broadcasts. Nevertheless, the majority of the time your order may fill at a higher level.

Patience is definitely required in situations where levels change drastically from up to down or from down to up. What I usually like to do is to wait for the price level to settle before buying right at the open. This method allows me time to do my homework. News broadcasts are part of that homework which will bring about decisions on what stocks to buy or sell. When good news has been out for a long time (either the night before or early morning,) the information provided will already be reflected

143

in the opening stock price. This truth is, all the optimism is already placed into a stock's price. Keep in mind that when the news comes out; placing a market order to buy the shares shortly thereafter will position you in a momentum-buying situation. Later, buyers may bid up the price of your shares in most circumstances.

When buying stocks, consider the theory of buying low and selling high. This excellent theory shall lead you on the path of buying shares on a dip and selling those shares into a rally. Another situation that is known to move stock prices is a merger or acquisition. Mergers and acquisitions affect stock prices also. Can you guess which way the stock prices usually head after a merger or an acquisition? The answer is not surprising; the acquired company usually rallies to new levels, while the acquiring company usually pulls back some from its trading level. The acquired company purchased at a premium would probably rise. While the acquiring company may have to put out some excess cash flow for the acquisition; therefore, gives back a little. In today's marketplace, many of the larger companies are swallowing up the smaller ones in order to either expand business or in order to attempt cornering the market.

CHAPTER 22:
DOLLAR COST AVERAGING

Dollar cost averaging is a simple means of investing. It is very simple to understand and requires no guesswork or homework on your part. Now doesn't that sound like something right up your alley?

One of the benefits of dollar cost averaging is that a lot of money is not required at one specific point in time (this is also more good news.) An individual can invest a small sum of money over a longer period and on a consistent basis. Some people like to invest on a monthly basis into a stock or mutual fund. These people are the ones who sit down and write out an investment check each month when they pay their bills. The point of this theory is for you to be able to add on a consistent basis an accumulation of a stock by obtaining a wide array of prices that would average to cost less than the actual market price. Over the long run, expect average cost of purchases to be less than the current market value of the stock. The best way to do this is to place (on a constant basis) a certain amount of money into the market at evenly distributed points in time over a long number of years.

What the price of the stock is at the time you buy it should not make a big difference to you when you invest. Success comes when you can believe that over the long haul, the stock value will go above the average where you purchased it. Also, you should realize that success may take several years. This is a preferred method for some beginners. This is due to its simplicity and lack of knowledge needed to perform this task of acquiring money and stocks that are either holding their own, or making a small profit.

If you feel you will be making many purchases then it is imperative that you take into account your brokers' fees. Brokers charge fees for the executions unless you are investing in some sort of a mutual fund. Brokers usually do not charge for additional purchases when dollar cost averaging in a mutual fund. A good rule of thumb is to check with the brokerage house in which you are doing business before investing. Try to find out what their usual fees are.

Let us say you had an extra $300 a month to invest in company 'ABCD.' When you write out your bills at the end of the month, also plan to write out a check for $300 dollars to purchase shares of stock in a company of your choice (after analysis of course.) On every purchase, you will be buying a different number of shares due to the fluctuation in market price of the security. When the company's stock price is depressed, you will be buying a larger number of shares with your $300 dollars. When the stock price inflates, you will be purchasing a smaller number of shares at a higher price.

Can you see what is developing in this scenario? If you follow this method, you will constantly be buying a greater quantity of shares when the stock price is lower than when it is higher. A question to ask yourself would be; "What time are you wasting or devoting to studying into the value of the security in your busy schedule?" Answer: "The time it takes you to write out a check. "

Personally, as an investor, I do not prefer this method. However, you may find the method suitable for yourself or for another individual that lacks time or knowledge. You may want to start out with this method and then move on into other methods later. Use this method to be able to do trading and learn the stock market business.

I used to work at a chain that had an employee stock purchase plan which deducted a certain percentage of my pay each week in order to invest the money back into the company's security. This would be a perfect example of dollar cost averaging. No matter what the price of the stock was at the end of the week, the action the company took with my money, ended up purchasing me a few shares. Over a longer period, these few numbers of shares would have accumulated to high levels and my average cost of purchases would be lower than the current market price.

Let us take the example of the $300 invested monthly over a period of six months. Try to understand exactly what is happening while it develops month after month. The illustration below (when studied) draws a clearer picture in your mind as to what has happened.

MONTH

	1	2	3	4	5	6
Invested	$300	$300	$300	$300	$300	$300
Price Value	8.5	13.6	7.5	8.6	10	12
Shares Purchased	35.29	22.06	40	34.88	30	25

Notice how when the price dropped to $7.5, that the highest amount of shares were purchased. When the price shot up to $13.6, the least amount of shares were purchased. The last price that the market valued our shares at was $12. Up until this point, we invested $1,800 and accumulated 187.23 shares. The average cost at which we purchased our shares came out to be $10.03 (the sum of all price values divided by 6.) The current market price of our shares has now become $12. Can you begin to see how this method works? Our average cost fell almost two full dollars below our current market price. We have already begun to see some extra value in this process so far.

CHAPTER 23:
MUTUAL FUNDS

Mutual funds are a great means of diversification. I suggest that you study the specific goals of each in order to determine your suitability. Some vastly diversified funds have a specific goal in mind, while others deal in certain sectors. Mutual funds may divide like stocks into aggressive growth, income, and a combination of the two. Funds may even contain bonds, government securities, or foreign securities. Some funds may also contain a combination of any one of these plus stocks. Younger individuals may prefer a growth mutual due to their time horizon. Then there are those individuals who prefer a more stable fund.

Owning mutual funds is a way to own stock in many companies all with one investment. By purchasing the shares of a mutual fund, you may be the owner of stock in up to thirty or more companies at once. Each fund makes up a different percentage of the portfolio. A beginning investor may purchase mutual funds due to its diversification and ability to own shares in an already managed fund.

Some mutual funds have fund managers that take care of all the investment decisions for you. I suggest you study and attempt analyzing the prospectus of each fund in order to provide yourself the fund manager's goals for the fund assigned to him. At the very least, study and get familiar with the stocks you own. Take a glance at all the companies that are in the fund you decide upon and attempt to analyze all of the funds that are in your portfolio.

The following questions are important ones to ask yourself before you make a final decision: Are you familiar with any of the funds you are thinking about purchasing? Do these funds suit your long-term goals?

Keep in mind, most mutual funds are long-term investments. Therefore, the challenge here is to think of each of the funds you invest in as a long-term investment. If you cannot decide on the exact sector you wish to invest in (growth, income, international) then you can choose to invest in index funds instead. Index funds perform like a mutual fund that mimics an index. Indexes purchased, as this may be the Dow or NASDAQ. Other funds also carry other indexes. A money market fund is also available which is considered one of the most stable funds to purchase.

Mutual funds trade almost the same way stocks trade. However, instead of a broker's trade fee, they may have sales charges such as management fees or advertisement fees. These two different types of fees are usually calculated as part of the sales percentage. The lower the fee obviously the better. Before purchasing funds, make sure that you know all the charges attached to your purchase or at the very least all the charges that could possibly be presented to you on your trade. You must also track the past growth record of the fund to make sure the fund manager has a great growth record.

The price of the mutual fund's share depends on its net asset value sometimes abbreviated as the fund's NAV. At the end of the business day is usually when prices calculate in order to determine the new NAV. The mutual funds NAV appreciates and depreciates similar to a single stock. Depending on the individual fund, a sales charge may or may not exist. If you purchase shares directly from a mutual fund company, you can avoid brokerage fees if the fund has no sales charge added. Some mutual funds require a minimum investment to take part in ownership of their shares. Individual investors should be able to maintain these minimum requirements before thinking about investing funds that they need for daily living expenses. Unlike stock's shares, mutual fund shares can be purchased in dollar amounts not in proportion to its share price or net asset value. If you invest $100 and decide 8 shares will complete most of your sale, you can actually purchase 8.75 to use the whole $100. It is possible to own 123.25 shares of a mutual fund. This is what makes it easy to invest a fixed dollar amount into funds on a monthly or quarterly basis without having to worry about how many shares you can purchase.

Okay, let us now try to understand this method by practicing buying a mutual fund. We have investigated a fund and found that it does suit our goals. We would prefer to invest a cool $10,000. The fund states it has a 4% sales load on it. In other words, the fund managers are going to charge us 4% of what we invest in the fund as fees for either buying our shares or for the managing costs of the securities in the fund. The $10,000 invested will only have the actual purchasing power of $9,600 dollars. The $400 difference will cover the sales charge of the fund. If the net asset value of these shares is $10.00, we will own 960 shares of the fund.

When we get charged initially for entering a fund, it is said to have a front-end load or a sales charge. Not all funds have front-end loans. Some have what are called back-end loads. These are fees paid when exiting your investment or selling shares. This usually occurs for selling a fund early. It rather serves as a penalty for exiting the fund. The longer you are invested, the better it becomes for you penalty wise. The majority of the fees go to the management services your fund manager supplies.

There is also a fund known as a 'no load fund'. In these funds, there are no sales charges whatsoever if you buy through the fund itself instead of using a broker. Unmanaged funds have no fees attached. As with any investment, you must always monitor it yourself. I would prefer a no load fund but depending on the individual and their commitment time to the investment, a load fund may also be appropriate.

Some fund managers charge fees to help their marketing costs. As with any purchase, you need to make sure you read the prospectus so you do not get hit with any surprise or unexpected fees.

CHAPTER 24:
OPTIONS

The following chapter presents a brief overview of options. Warning, many concepts will be left out. Options are risky and it is easier to lose your original investment with options than the other methods on the marketplace today. Therefore, this section is being presented for the more experienced investors. With options, you gain the right to buy or sell a stock without actually owning the stock at the time you place the option order. However, what you are purchasing is the option to do so at a future time.

The option strategy leverages your buying power. Options allow you to purchase a stock somewhere down the line, without actually owning any shares at the present time. This grants you the ability to take advantage of any future price swings in the stock. In order to buy 100 shares of a stock that is trading at $88, you would have to pay $8,800. By purchasing an option for 100 shares of the same stock, it may only end up costing you $1000. This amount will vary depending upon what the options price is. The option price is determined by a time value and the amount the stock that is 'in the money.'

When an option is in the money, it means that you can obtain capital gains when you execute an option, or when you actually sell it. When an option is 'out of the money,' you will find you have no capital gains, when either executing your option or selling it.

Options have an expiration date or period in time when they expire. You must make your decision based on whether you want to purchase your shares, sell your option, or let the option expire. When an option is allowed to expire, chances are you are 'out of money.' At this time (expiration,) you will gain no benefit in purchasing it, or selling it earlier. The more an option is 'in the money,' and the more time value remaining before expiration, the more the option is worth. The more an option is 'out of the money' and the less remaining time there is before expiration, the less your option is worth.

It is possible to purchase options on a number of stocks and even indexes. Later, you can purchase the option to either buy a stock or sell a stock later. If you have made up your mind that you believe a stock price will rise (being bullish) or appreciate, you can buy a 'call'. If you believe a stock's price will decrease or depreciate (being bearish) in value, you can buy a 'put'. The point or price where you can purchase an option is a 'strike price'. The Exchange Board predetermines the strike prices, depending upon the price of the stock. The strike price may or may not be trading exactly where the current market value of the stock is trading. Strike prices may be above or below the stock's actual market value at that particular time.

Take for example, a stock trading at $34. Strike prices for this stock may exist at $30 or $40. This will mean that you can buy an option at these prices. When you buy a 'call', you could also say you are 'long the security.' On the other hand, when you buy a 'put,' you could say you are 'short the security.' Calls or puts can also be sold. This idea is more advanced but at the same time, there is some theory behind it.

For learning purposes, now we will discuss a few facts about buying a call or a put. Let us use them together as a strategy and do this at the same time.

Without taking into account how much it cost us to buy the option, we will see if our option is in or out of the money.

- $30 = strike price
- $34 = market value price
- $40 = strike price

Practice thinking about the following: If you were to buy a call at $30, how much do you believe you would we be spending if you deducted the cost for making the option? Realize too that you would not actually be charged this $30 at the time the call was placed. Again, when you buy a call, you take a long position and wish the price to appreciate. Let us say that the current market value of the stock is $34. Our established strike price or start point would be $30 [$34 - $30 = $4.] Now, you are in the money by $4 (the difference between the CMV and the strike price.) Keep in mind, you still have not accounted for the money it cost us to buy the option (fee.)

Ask yourself "If I bought a put at the strike price of $40, how much would I be in the money?" Remember in a put, you are short the position and you want the stock price to go down ($40-$34=$6.) You are $6 in the money in this situation.

Now, let us go a little further into understanding about options. What if you bought a call at the strike price of $40? In this case, you would be 'out of the money.' To be in the money, you would need a current market value of the stock above $40 (not accounting our costs yet for the purchase.)

To be in the money, you would need a current market value of the stock to be above $40 (not accounting our costs yet for the purchase.) With the market price above $40, calls are in the money and puts are out of the money. According to the diagram below, you are now $6 out of the money.

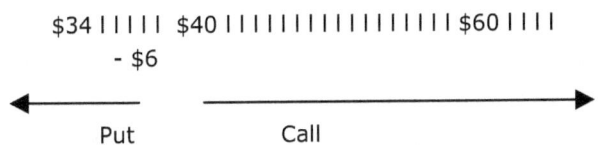

$34 I I I I I $40 I I I I I I I I I I I I I I I I I $60 I I I I
    - $6

Put   Call

At this time, I hope that you are following along and ready to take the discussion of options a bit further. Now look at the question, "If you had purchased a put at $30, would you have been out of the money. In this case you would have been out of the money by $4 ($34 - 30 = $4.)

The price of an option is based on its premium. The premium represents its' 'in the money,' or 'out of the money,' status and also the time period remaining before expiration. Let us say the premium for 'ABCD' stock is $4; and, the strike price is $20. To buy a hundred shares of 'ABCD' outright, would cost you $2000 if the market value were also $20. To buy one call option of this company's stock (100 shares,) would cost you only $400 (100 shares x $4 premium = $400.) You now control 'ABCD's ability of price fluctuation for a much cheaper price.

For a minute let us go back to the 'in' and 'out of the money' options in order to consider your cost for buying the option. It is very important to add this cost into your calculation in order to determine what your break-even point will be. In buying a call, you want the stock price to rise above $20. Since it cost you a $4 dollar premium to purchase this option, you must at least reach $20 (strike price) + $4 (premium) = $24 just to break even. Profits are seen once you overcome your breakeven point of $24.

Let us say that at a $20 strike price, you purchased a put for the premium of $3 costing you a total of $300.

One option is equal to a hundred shares; two options are equal to 200 shares and so on.

What do you believe your breakeven point will be now? In a put, we want the price to go downward below $20. Taking the $3 premium into account or even our cost of $300 (3x100,) our breakeven point will be $17. In order for you to gain in this position, the stock price must drop below $17. The most you can lose in buying a call or a put is your cost that you paid for the premium.

Say your stock in the above example climbs to $30. Your put is out of the money by 10 points above the strike price and 13 points above your cost. You would not lose $1000 or $1300 in this instance. Your original $300 would be your maximum loss. When you buy a call or a put that falls out of the money the most you can lose is the premium. The most you can gain in buying a call is infinite. The stock price is capable of rising and rising to infinity. There is no limit to how high the price can rise before expiration. Since this does not happen in most situations, it is shown at this time to give you an idea of the limitless possibilities. The truth is what can be gained in a put is limited. The farthest a stock can fall down to is zero. So the most you can gain in buying a put is the strike price minus your premium cost.

Let us, for practice sake, take the following two examples and see what your capital gains might end up being:

Example 1:

Buy one call option of 'ABCD' at a strike price for $30 at a premium of $5. Let us say the stock soars to $55. What will your capital gains be? First, please take the time to consider the breakeven point. This option cost you $5 or $500 for one option. Your breakeven point will be $35 [$30 (strike price) + $5 (premium).] Anything above $35 will be a gain. The stock price soared to $55, $55 (current market price) - $35 (breakeven point) = $20. You have gained $20 a share value translating into a capital gain of $2000 ($20 x 100 shares or 1 option contract.)

Example 2:

Buy going a bit further; let us look at you buying one put option of 'ABCD' for a strike price of $50 for a premium of $7. The stock price plummets to $23. What do you believe your gains will be now? Find the breakeven point again ($50 - $7 = $43.) When buying a put, subtract the premium from the strike price in order to get the breakeven point. To determine gains, subtract the current market price from the breakeven point; $43 - $23 = $20. Again, you have gained $20 a share or $2000 for your total option of 100 shares.

Now, let us go over what has been presented thus far. For instance, in Example 1, what do you believe would have happened if the stock price had fallen to $2? What do you believe your total loss would have been? In this example, $2 is way out of the money. The truth is, no matter how far out of the money you were when you bought the call; the most you could lose would have been your premium. $5 x 100 shares (1 option) would have given you a loss of $500.

Let us now study Example 2 and see that if the stock price soared to $75, the loss would only have been the premium of $7 or $700 total for your 100 shares.

Buying calls and buying puts are two of the most basic concepts in options. Other order types exist in options but due to their high risk potential, let us not consider them any further. We will look at just one more simple strategy involving buying both a call and a put at the same strike price. This strategy is a 'long straddle.' The long straddle is a strategy used best when there is a period of high volatility in a stock price.

High P/E stocks similar to the ones in the Internet sector may have been great targets. If the stock prices do not fluctuate at the end of their expiration period, chances are you will be out of the money. Stocks with wide trading ranges deserve a second glance because this strategy. On the other hand, stocks with narrow trading ranges should be discarded when using this approach. It is important to make back the money spent on purchasing a call as well as the money spent on a put.

Example 3:

Let us look at an example of a long straddle. The strike price for 'ABCD' is $200. The stock's current market value is $192. Your option expires in three months with a call premium of $5 and a put premium of $10. Think about what you believe your gain would be if the stock price skyrocketed to $285? One contract's option cost in a long straddle will be the total of the call, plus the puts premium prices.

As you can see, we need to make more points in stock price value to cover the option. First, look at the breakpoints. Since you purchased both a call and a put, you will have two breakeven points. Your breakeven point to the downside would be $200 – ($10 + $5 = $15 sum of premiums) = $185. Your breakeven point to the upside then would be $200 + ($10 + $5 = $15) = $215. In this situation, you will be 'in the money' if the stock's price is less than $185 or more than $215. In this circumstance, you were in the money by $70 (285 - 215.) Your total gain would be $7000 for an initial investment of $1500. With $1500, you can control a $192 stock's ability to make money by fluctuating in market value.

A large increase in stock price or a large decrease in price would allow for capital gains. You do not however have to know exactly which way the price is moving. Nevertheless, you do need to hope that the price moves. The only problem with options is the risk potential of falling out of the money. When this happens, you will lose the original investment. Calls and puts can also be bought on indexes.

During the recent days of September 2001, the DOW industrial averages fell sharply in a single week. An Investor buying puts at that time would have made substantial money. Making money can be all about timing or guessing which way a company is heading to the upside or to downside. Other strategies exist where you can even make money when a stock trades in the same trading range for a long period of time. For our purposes we will avoid options and concentrate on making value investments instead.

CHAPTER 25:
BONDS

Another investment tool people tend to use is bonds. Bonds may not have the growth potential of common stocks. However, bonds are still a great way to invest in a fixed income security. Bonds provide constant income over a long period.

For example sake, pretend you have two friends named Bill and Bob. Bill and Bob usually deal with one another on a constant basis regarding money matters. Bill who is in a bad economic situation has luckily discovered what he believes to be a great way to make some extra money. Sadly, though Bill does not have enough capital to make the discovery happen in his present economic condition.

One day, Bill spoke to Bob explaining how he felt they both could get rich by a lucky discovery that he had made. After listening to Bill for an hour, he began to believe the discovery might bring a profit so he quickly informed Bill, "Do not worry, I will lend you the $1,000 needed in order to get this investment started." Bill, very pleased over the loan, told Bob, "Well, Bob in return for this loan, I will give you an 8% interest return yearly. I will repay you in payment portions twice yearly until the end of the year when I pay you back the total amount of money owed." All seemed fair to both men. Hence, Bob lent the $1,000 to Bill. Six months later, Bill paid Bob the first payment of interest of $40 due on the loan. For the entire year, Bob made $80 total interest from two payments of $40 twice a year. At the end of the year, Bob should have had his $1,000 back, along with a $40 interest payment, for a total of $1,040 as his last payment. Bob's total return of $1,080 at year-end is the initial promised 8% return. That does not sound too complicated, now does it?

Bonds tend to work the same way as the explanation above. A bond is money lent from one source to another with an interest rate of return earned on the loaned money until the lender's loan is paid. The $1,000 represents the 'par value' of the bond. The interest amount is the 'coupon rate' of the bond. The year period (length of the loan) is the 'maturity date' when you receive back your original capital investment.

The easiest way to picture a bond is as an investor loaning money to a person representing a company, government, or municipality. Depending upon what type of bond we will be investing in will actually determine how likely you are able to get back your money lent. A company (or other bond issuer) may default in bad economic times and then your money may not be totally 100% guaranteed to be repaid. That is why it is important to invest in issuers that will be more likely to repay your capital investment. Rating services exist that place a ranking on the bonds that exist to purchase. It would be a wise decision to investigate into these ranking systems before purchasing any bonds. The better the bond rating of the issuer, the better the value of the bond. If the issuer of the bond cannot repay you back the value of the bond then the value of the bond will fall drastically to junk status.

As a purchaser of a bond, you are classified as a creditor of the company. In case of a liquidation situation, creditors will have priority over stockholders in their order of payment. Government treasury bonds such as t-bills, t-notes, or t-bonds may provide a safer haven for your money than certain companies because the government backs them. These bonds only differ in their time of maturity.

Besides the financial status of the company, the number one influence on bonds (in my opinion) is the current interest rate. Bonds and interest rates have an inverse relationship to one another. When interest rates go down, the value of your bond rises. When interest rates rise, the value of your bond drops. "Why is this?" you may ask? Well let us now take another look at the example above to investigate the answer to this question.

One thing we know for sure is that Bob lent Bill the money at an 8% interest rate for a period of one year. Over the period of that year, the interest rates may have fluctuated to the upside or the downside depending upon the federal reserve board. Now let us surmise that the federal reserve board decided to lower the interest rates from 8% to 7.5%. What do you believe will happen to the price of the bond? The majority of the public will now be receiving at 7.5% rate while Bob will still be receiving his comfortable 8% rate of return. This will surely increase the value of his bond. What if the interest rates were to rise half a percentage point (50 basic points)? Bob would not be as comfortable as he was before the change. He would be receiving an 8% return on his money while the rest of the community would be receiving 8.5% back on their money yearly. Bob's bond price would surely drop.

Bonds usually sell in $1000 lots. However, bonds can vary depending on the issuer of the bond. Maturity dates of the bond can vary also. They can go from six months, one year, ten years, or even thirty years depending again upon the issuer and type of bond. In the example of the bond above, the interest rate rose above the coupon rate of 8%. At its end, the bond will likely trade below the $1000 dollar original investment. This drop will be due to its lower return now. This bond as compared to other issuers with newer higher interest rate coupons attached to them will have a lower return. This bond is now considered as being traded at a discount because its value will be a tad below $1000. In the situation where the interest rate dropped below the coupon rate, the value of that bond will end up being worth a tad more than the rest. That bond actually should trade at a premium.

The truth is the price of the bond can rise above or fall below the $1000 par value. Therefore, a good question to ask in order to understand bonds is, "How are the bond prices quoted?" The natural answer would be that bond prices are quoted in percentages of the original investment at par value. A bond trading at a premium may quote at $110 or 110% of par value of $1000. This premium bond will then trade at $1100 [$1000 x .10 = $100 (premium value) + $1000 = $1100]. A bond trading at a discount may have a value of $93 or 93% of par value of $1000. This discount bond will be trading at $930 [$1000 x .07 = $70 (discount value,) $1000 - $70 = $930.] A simpler calculation would be for you to just multiply the $1000 par value by the percentage of par of 93% or $.93 to attain your value of $930 (1000 x $.93 = $930.)

The examples above take into consideration the premium and discount values for your understanding of the exercise. As stated earlier, bonds are a way to attain fixed income in a portfolio. People tend to have both stocks and bonds in their portfolio in order to balance the portfolio between equity and fixed income securities. 'At par value' means when interest rates and the bond rates stay the same. Par value also means when the yield on the bond is equal to the initial coupon rate. In the case above, the yield was the constant 8%.

What happens when the interest rates change? Will the bond still be yielding the constant 8% fixed return rate? The yield of our bonds will be affected depending on whether or not our bond is trading at a discount or a premium. With an 8% coupon rate, no matter what happens, you will receive the $80 a year, but the yield might not necessarily be 8%. Maybe the bond was trading at a premium of $110 when you purchased it. That being true, "What would be your yield at the current price?" The purchase price would be $1100 and you would receive $80 a year with this purchase. Just as we have calculated dividend yields before, we can calculate the current bond yield:

$$\frac{\$\ \ 80}{\$1100} = 7.27\% \text{ as our current yield}$$

This value is lower than the coupon rate, because the bond was purchased at a higher price. Due to the fact you bought the bond at a premium, the coupon rate of 8% would yield only 7.27%.

Now, I am going to ask you a few more questions in order to help you understand bonds. "What might occur if you bought the bond at a discount of 10% instead of at a premium of 10%? How would that affect your current yield? If you purchased the bond at $900 with a 8% coupon rate what would be your current yield then?" The answer of "The $80 will be your fixed income and will not change due to your coupon rate" makes most sense; look below to see how this maps out:

$$\frac{\$\ \ 80}{\$900} = 8.89\% \text{ as our current yield}$$

Another question to contemplate at this time is: "Can you see what the difference buying at a premium or buying at a discount can mean to your yield at the current time of purchase?" The answer to this question would be "From this example, you can conclude that price and yields have inverse relationships to one another." As the market price of the bond falls, it yields higher than its coupon rate. As the market price of the bond increases, it yields lower than its coupon rate.

Let us go a step deeper into the subject of bond yields. One important fact to know is that you need to take into account the difference the yields receive at the end of the life of the bond or maturity date. This method adds the premium that you paid to your losses or the discount received towards your gains. This is known as the 'yield to maturity' for the bond. When buying a bond at a premium, your yield to maturity will be less than your current yield. When buying a bond at a discount, your yield to the maturity date will be higher than your current yield. This difference happens because you bought the bond at a bargain price.

Using the situation above, one thing you also need to understand thoroughly is that you had an original coupon rate of 8%. You purchased the bond at a discount of $900 yielding 8.89% at the time. A question to contemplate in this situation would be "If the bond had a 1-year maturity date, what do you believe your actual yield to maturity would be at the end of the year?" To answer this question, first let us determine the actual gain. One fact you now know for sure is that as long as the company pays the yield and stays healthy, you will receive your $80.

One of the last things you need to take into account is that the gain you received was from buying low. You managed to pick up an extra $100 from buying this bond as low as $1000 - $900 = $100. By maturity, you will have paid $1000 for the bond that was the par value for the bond. The end total gain will be the total of your $80 from the interest and the $100 from your discount equaling $180.

Take the time to consider what your yield to maturity might be equaling now?

$$\frac{\$80(\text{due to coupon}) + \$100(\text{due to discount})}{\$900 \ (\text{your purchase price})} = 20\% \text{ yield to maturity}$$

Take note, bonds can be called or purchased back by the issuer before the actual maturation date. This can affect yields. What I most wanted you, the trader, to learn by this chapter is; if you are looking for a means of diversification in a fixed income pathway, bonds may be a choice for your consideration.

CHAPTER 26:
REAL ESTATE

Real estate investments may also not be a bad choice during a period of economic downturn. An economic downturn would be the time to consider purchasing a house. When the economy takes a turn for the worse, chances are you will see interest rates fall substantially. Lower interest rates make purchasing that house you have always wanted a much better bargain. The loan will be easier to acquire when interest rates are low.

Refinancing a house loan in a period of low interest rates is also a wise choice. This is especially true when it is a house which was financed and locked in at a higher interest rate. Another real estate idea might be acquiring a bargain on a house that has been on the market for a long time that consumers have shown no interest in due to consumer sentiment. Take advantage of lower interest rates and place a lower bid on a house than its actual retail estimated value. See if you become the new owner.

Just like a securities price, a real estate purchase may also be bought at a discount by negotiating with the sellers. Sellers are often willing to budge if they are simply asked. Circumstances may have arisen in the seller's lives where the money is needed fast and they may be willing to sell their house for a cheaper price. It could be that they are moving to a new location and just want a fast sale. The sellers may even be under a severe circumstance such as a death in the family and need to sell the estate. I would like to suggest placing a bid lower than their asking price. Even if the price is substantially lower than their asking price, you can raise the price later. If you make a higher bid to start, there is usually no turning back. Asking high amounts to begin with will set you in a trap.

Real estate investing is of course not a sure thing like anything is in life. Sometimes, by investing in real estate, people seem to have a sense of security. Owning something like real estate can make an individual feel as if they are more successful. If the value of the real estate goes up or down it will always be there. The same thing cannot be said about too many stocks these days. A real estate owner can actually see what he has purchased and touch it with his senses. When purchasing securities, it is not possible to see the actual purchased product.

If the idea of making money by purchasing real estate interests you, investigate further by looking in a local paper and trying to find an advertisement for a listing of houses that are undergoing foreclosure. These lists may help you obtain a bargain price for a house. An ordinary real estate broker would not be showing you these houses. Auctions also exist for houses and the money they usually cost is very low. I believe it would be fun to show up for an auction on a house some rainy day when nobody else seems to want to purchase the house. You may find that you are the only person bidding on the house in some severe situations. It is always worth a shot to look into appealing auctions on houses.

For investing purposes, I would suggest to purchase a house you only believe will rise in value in the future years. Only purchase a house that you feel is already a bargain. Make sure the asked purchase price for the property at that time does suit your needs. Make a decision that holds within itself that even if you cannot sell the house right away to make a profit, you are financially safe still owning the property. In bad economical times, you may not be able to find a buyer for a long time.

I suggest always look at every aspect of the purchase and then determine what financial shape you might be in if the worst happens. If you cannot sell the house in a year, will you be in big trouble? Now consider for a moment, and analyze the complete picture of owning the real estate and if you have any doubts, avoid the purchase. Another thing one can do with purchased real estate is to hold on to the house for a long period of time and build equity in the house. Using your equity as an advantage in obtaining another loan and buying more additional pieces of property is a good financial decision. However, be careful in this type of decision making and do not overextend yourself.

Like in our stock section, I dislike using margin to purchase securities. When purchasing a property you also need to take into consideration the forced taxes paid per year on top of your mortgage costs. Some areas have higher taxes than others do. Try to make sure you know how much your taxes are going to be before making any purchases. Different areas also may have different values for the same house according to its area value. The same house in a farmland area may be only a quarter of the cost of the same house in a higher-class wealthy community. Before jumping into a purchase, get a feel for the areas retail value.

As a security has a balance sheet, a house has a sheet of paper that lists all the rooms contained in the house along with its tax price per year. One important figure found on this sheet, if you are not familiar with the area or going price for houses, is an estimated value number. This may list the value of the house separate from the value of the land and give you a total value number. Just like in securities, you may want to refer to this value of the house similar to the securities book value. Analyze the situation thoroughly. See if you can purchase the property for

170

less than this price. You may find you have received a slight bargain for the house. It will at least give you a better idea of the value range of the house. You may not want to sell the real estate at all.

Most people use their properties as a source of income by receiving rentals from their properties or units. This is a great way to help you to pay off the mortgage and to pay the taxes for the year. Having money left over after the expenses are paid will help to achieve a nice income property. This will help to increase your bankroll over time while helping you place more equity into your house. As with all rentals, you will have expenses when things break. Expenses are always a surprise when the plumbing or roofing requires replacing. Please consider all these type of costs before making any investment ventures.

CHECKLIST

1. ☐   P/E preferably < 15
2. ☐   Yield preferably > 5%
3. ☐   Earnings per share (must be positive and consistent over time)
4. ☐   ROE Return on Equity > 20% (management effectiveness to invest it's profits)
5. ☐   P/S Price to Sales
6. ☐   Book Value
7. ☐   Debt to Equity preferably < 1 (the lower the better)
8. ☐   Beta Value (stable stocks have lower values)
9. ☐   Observe the 52-week range (for a feel of where it's trading)
10. ☐ Growth Rate > P/E
11. ☐ PEG < 1
12. ☐ Profits > 10% minimum
13. ☐ Is their value in the brand name?
14. ☐ Consistent increase in earnings
15. ☐ Consistent increases in dividends over the years
16. ☐ Current and Quick ratios show no sign of inventory build up
17. ☐ You understand the company and how it works
18. ☐ Volume > 100,000 shares daily